DONKEYS (

By the same author:
The Irish Donkey

DONKEYS GALORE

by

AVERIL SWINFEN

David & Charles

Newton Abbot   London   North Pomfret (VT)   Vancouver

ISBN 0 7153 7150 9

Library of Congress Catalog Card Number 76-2883

© Averil Swinfen 1976

All rights reserved. No part of this publication may be reproduced, stored in a retrieval system, or transmitted, in any form or by any means, electronic, mechanical, photocopying, recording or otherwise, without the prior permission of David & Charles (Publishers) Limited

Set in 12 on 13pt Bembo
and printed in Great Britain
by Latimer Trend & Company Ltd Plymouth
for David & Charles (Publishers) Limited
Brunel House Newton Abbot Devon

Published in the United States of America
by David & Charles Inc
North Pomfret Vermont 05053 USA

Published in Canada
by Douglas David & Charles Limited
1875 Welch Street North Vancouver BC

Contents

	Acknowledgements	6
	Foreword	7
1	Carried Away	9
2	Life Among the Donkeys	16
3	On the Menu	36
4	Twinnies	49
5	Open to the Public	61
6	Fair Winds and Foul Weather	76
7	Our Animal 'Stars'	91
8	On with the Show	102
9	Outward Bound	115
10	Our Duty to Animals	126
	Index	134

To my husband Carol, with love

Faobhar, gaoth, agus gràdh, tri nithe nà feictear go bràth.
Three things that are never seen – a blade's edge, wind and love.
A Miscellany of Irish Proverbs
Collected and edited by Thomas F. O'Rahilly

I am truly grateful to Dr L. B. O'Moore, MSc, PhD, MRCVS, MRIA, Associate Director of the Agricultural Institute, Dublin, for his interest and help on many occasions and for his kindness in preparing for this book the advice in Chapter 3. To Dr Patrick Power, MB, DPM, FRCPsye of Our Lady's Hospital, Ennis, County Clare, I tender my respectful admiration for breaking new ground in making his hospital the first to use our donkeys in therapeutic work; and my sincere thanks to him for permission to publish his report on their effect.

I am indebted to Mrs Daphne Kingsley-Lewis for giving me leave to quote from her paper entitled 'Skeletal Structure of the Donkey compared with the Horse'. Also to the Hon Mrs E. Agnew for allowing me to repeat part of her letter to me about the foal who declined to suck. I also thank the *Los Angeles Times* for their permission to reprint the story attributed to them in Chapter 9.

My daughter Coral Knowles has done the delightful drawings which cleverly portray events and ideas referred to in this book. For these and for typing the manuscript I am deeply grateful to her. To my husband Carol, who gave all the help I could not have done without goes my heartfelt thanks. For putting me up and for putting up with me during my visits to the publishers I thank my brother Langley Humphreys and his wife Rosemary.

Foreword

The donkey is one of our most intriguing domesticated animals. For his success in resisting total submission and enslavement to our various demands, he has been unfairly rebuked as dull, obstinate and stupid. But the donkey has his own point of view and will do what he wants when he wants. His independence is refreshing in an age of increasing monotony brought about by conformity and harmonisation.

The donkey's role in our society is rapidly evolving from that of a beast of burden to becoming one of the most charming, cuddly and affectionate pets. I personally mourn their disappearance from the landscape as a working animal and as part of the agrarian culture. However, nothing can be done about this.

With the changing role of the donkey and increasing public interest in it as a pet, there is now a great demand for books and information on donkeys. Indeed for some time I have been looking for such a book. Therefore the arrival of *Donkeys Galore* is highly appropriate.

Averil Swinfen returned to her native Ireland many years ago and settled at Spanish Point in County Clare. To the visitor, the area is outstanding: a dramatic rocky and grass-topped coastline subjected to the full ferocity of Atlantic storms. It is also a landscape of green pastures, bogland and small farms; the friendly towns of Miltown Malbay and Ennistymon, and above all, a countryside in which the donkey still works alongside man. Here the rasping calls of corncrakes and the somewhat mournful 'hehaw' of donkeys reverberate throughout the landscape. In this setting, overcoming all the problems created by geographical isolation, Averil Swinfen has created a highly successful donkey stud.

Her book is a frank and often humorous account of her life and

FOREWORD

experiences with donkeys galore. For anybody contemplating breeding and rearing donkeys the book is essential reading. The chapters on donkey husbandry contain information which only comes from years of dedicated concern with donkeys. Visitors to her Spanish Point donkey stud and their reactions to donkeys provide amusing diversion to the day-to-day work.

Throughout her work Averil Swinfen has been deeply concerned with raising the status of the donkey and reducing cruelty and ill-treatment. She was instrumental in establishing the Irish Donkey Society which successfully persuaded the Royal Dublin Society to hold donkey classes at the world famous horse show held each year in Dublin.

Donkeys Galore is a lively and humorous book which will not only be enjoyed by other donkey enthusiasts but also by people with a broad interest in our country life.

David Cabot
April 1976

1 Carried Away

Of all animal companions it would be hard to find one more versatile or long-lasting than the donkey. At home in, or adaptable to, most places, it has a life expectancy of thirty years or more; from authoritative sources I have even heard instances of donkeys living to be fifty or sixty years old. Much depends on how carefully they have been looked after, although most donkeys require only the rational considerations of sustenance, companionship and help in sickness or when aged.

Those who assume that the ass is the embodiment of dullness, stupidity and sloth, simply because for some inexplicable reason that view has been passed down from one generation to another, need but a short acquaintance with any donkey to realise that this commonly held belief is far from the truth. We who live surrounded by these animals recognise them as the most intriguing and entertaining of creatures. If, on occasion, that entertainment is marred by some tiresome behaviour, this nearly always turns out to have been actuated by man's stupidity, such as someone forgetting to close the gate or the stable door so that the donkeys stray into the garden and eat the vegetables.

The donkey's accomplishments are mostly what its master chooses to teach it, and this will obviously vary according to the owner's requirements and the animal's age, sex and size. Its range of perception is acute and its enurement to man is easily established. The behavioural chain in the animal will, therefore, reflect to a great extent that of its human owner or instructor. And it is this very same ability to reflect its master's desires which has enabled the ass to be of paramount importance to the human race. No other animal has been stitched into the tapestry of man's life with such a wealth of pattern. From my window here I see him plodding up the lane with a cart-load of seaweed; then again, he appears ambling along with a load of hay. On the bogs not far away he is still bringing in the turf for next winter's fires and, though lorries and tractors do most of the carrying today, there are still places where only a donkey can go. From another window I see him giving rides to children and trotting down the drive with the trap full of tourists. In the paddock the foals dance about and preen themselves whilst fields away on the sea-sky line the stallions graze, pausing every now and again to emit their awesome bray.

But let us look back a little to the donkeys' heyday in the British Isles when they were kept, often as luxuries, by well-to-do Victorian and Edwardian families, being ridden and driven in various vehicles, as the illustrations and photographs from books, magazines and photograph albums of those eras reveal. Then, as new and exciting ways of movement evolved in the shape of tricycles, bicycles and automobiles, the interest in the donkey dwindled, as also did the usefulness of the horse for ordinary transport.

I have often wondered why, over the succeeding years, so few animal-minded people have rediscovered the delightful, lovable qualities of the donkey. Indeed the general public of today is hardly yet aware of the ass's existence, other than as an animal used by less affluent members of society in many countries, or by employing its name in facetious abuse. Yet practically without exception, noted travellers of over a century ago or more who wrote about the wild ass gave glowing accounts of its beauty, courage, agility and graceful deportment when encountered in its natural environment. And those people who had the opportunity of getting to know asses better, made mention of their traits of friendliness, curiosity, extremely knowing ways and their avid bid for affectionate attention and fondling, though one of the species was known to be less tractable and of a shyer disposition.

Not many people who admired the wild ass in its natural habitats would want to capture and retain it, other than for sending to zoos, as the horse was more easily procurable to supply the demand of the day for strength and speed. When regarding the somewhat chastened descendants of these fine creatures which over the years have degenerated by living in unsuitable climatic conditions, suffering ill-treatment and inbreeding, it seems to me that the purely modest regard for the domestic ass until recent years is a typical result of that common mistake of judging the book by the cover!

Another factor is that, except for young children who keep pets which are easy to care for, and adults who want a dog or cat for companionship, the majority of people who go in for any kind of animal, make the ill-founded assumption that they must do so for some exciting or profitable reason according to their social status, enthusiasms or purse-strings. This being true it is easy to see how poor, forlorn-looking Neddy, plodding slowly and calmly along with his everyday work, would not merit a place in many people's picture of life.

Luckily times are changing and I'm very glad that the donkey stepped into my picture, or – more accurately – that I stepped into his! Collecting and breeding donkeys was certainly not in my mind when I returned to my native Ireland about twelve years ago.

As children we had taken little notice of these quiet grey and brown neighbours. The donkeys had their own work to do and what energy they had left over was a bit on the slow side for us tear-aways, too full of the impatience of youth to discern their potential in other directions. They were just a part of life around us, in the same category as the other domestic animals living on a sheltered inland farm, well-fed, watered and not subject to more than the ordinary maladies that occur everywhere where there are living creatures.

Returning to Ireland we made our home at Spanish Point, County Clare, so-called because of its association with the Spanish Armada of 1588. Many Spanish sailors were drowned in these western Atlantic waters when their storm-tossed ships failed the challenge of the elements. Survivors who landed in the vicinity were put to death by order of the then governor of the province of Connaught, and tradition also records that they were buried in fields around the district. Now, nearly 400 years later, instead of the cries of those luckless sailors, the strident brays of our donkeys disturb the quiet scene, although at first I did not envisage keeping any outdoor animals on such unsheltered land and deemed looking after them impossible for me.

Spanish Point lies midway along the Clare coast where coastal scenery is at its best and most varied, a treasure trove of picturesque and historical settings. Here, the unsuspecting visitor can travel for days in brilliant sunshine along the north-western seaside road at the foot of grey limestone stepped hills, through the unique stone-filled district called the Burren, where myriads of wild Alpine flowers bloom, to the famous Cliffs of Moher which tower 700ft above the sea. The route goes on past sandy beaches, small calm coves and villages decorated with drying seaweed, through pleasant farmland and seaside towns. It continues along the southern peninsula to the mouth of the river Shannon, through moorland to where, far below, the Atlantic swirls around and against the massive, and sometimes grotesquely formed, rocks.

The visitor will be more than happy with what he sees on these quiet and serene days, but should not be deluded into thinking our shores always have this unruffled mien. Among so much spectacular scenery not everyone notices the scarcity of sheltering trees and hedges. Stone walls are the dividing lines of fields and boundaries, many of them are low and built in a lace-like pattern so that the winds can push through the perforated structures with less chance of toppling them. On many other days the tourist will see this open country sodden with rainfall and apparently destitute of all comfort. For our western county seaboard can run almost the whole gamut of weather conditions and, when belaboured by Atlantic gales which tear around in undisciplined ferocity, it is easy to feel that it could dispatch both man and beast from off the face of the map with a kick from its southern foot-like extremity.

It is not, therefore, the best or the easiest place in the world to breed donkeys. This part of the northern hemisphere, so lacking in the dry and arid conditions in which most of their ancestors flourished, has only played host to these mammals for a few centuries. The species has survived but only at great cost to their numbers and physique. In areas which have a climate more like that of their natural habitat, such as parts of Australia and the USA, where their arrival is yet more recent, donkeys have thrived and multiplied. To breed them in our part of Ireland and other exposed places in the British Isles necessitates constant care and adjustment to meet the climatic conditions, something not always understood by those in inland districts containing more natural shelter from the wind and rain.

The man who goes out to study living creatures in their natural habitat will have to contend with many problems, but not this environmental one. It is the individual who studies them away from their natural home who must take such climatic factors into account, while differentiating at the same time between changes which affect the animal physically and those which affect it psychologically. It is also necessary to take into consideration the length of time since the beast or its ancestors left their natural home, especially when the change in environment involves a change in climate, as this makes adaptation more difficult and more lengthy. The greater the change, the greater will be the difficulty. That is why, if life were without other interests and commitments, save only an unconquerable ambition to devote it to the breeding and study of donkeys in an area conducive to their welfare, that area would not be the west coast of Ireland.

Yet, chance can favour us all in strange ways, and our choice of home has provided some fortuitous advantages. If I had chosen to breed donkeys in those sheltered places to which the animals were accustomed, I would never have gained the knowledge of them which the experiences of endeavouring to meet such environmental difficulties brought my way.

Keeping the donkeys in satisfactory condition, both inside and out, over a long stretch of bad weather more than doubles the attention they require at other times; both cattle and horses can take more punishment from such weather than the ass. During one time of appalling conditions both our stallions and mares proved less fertile, our usual worming programme, which is carried out four times a year, was increased, and it seemed that we were forever nervously on the lookout for lung worm, fluke and other wet-weather problems. Yet with the exception of one little white ass which died from the result of a chill turning to pneumonia, we literally weathered the storms without serious trouble. It has given me the courage to enlarge upon Aristotle's statement that asses will not live wild in a cold climate; I should like to add that they will not easily survive without shelter and care in an excessively windy and rainy climate.

All this theorising has led me to jump the gun, and I should here explain that having previously owned horses, cattle and pigs, with which I had become too emotionally involved, not for a moment did I ever think of getting back into 'animal life' in such a big way – perish the thought. Did I not know the ropes as far as animals *en masse* and myself were concerned, and were not the two poodles which I already owned all that was required? Yes, I suppose so, but what I did not take into account at that stage was the fascination of the donkey itself; its winning ways, intriguing habits and strange, sometimes bewildering individuality of behaviour, made it tantalisingly different from the pony and any other animal with which I had been closely associated.

From the moment I first decided to purchase two donkey mares I was lost. In those fathomless eyes, which over the trials of the centuries have observed us humans without seeing much to our credit where they were concerned, I sensed resignment to a life sentence without remittance. Hopefully this is not to be: it is said that everything comes to he who waits, and world-wide emancipation is waiting for *Equus asinus*. I only trust that our Irish venture contributes in some way towards this end.

2 Life Among the Donkeys

The advent of donkeys in our life certainly changed its pattern and involved us in much that had hitherto been foreign to it. We gained a little knowledge on a lot of subjects, seldom if ever before connected with donkeys: getting to know the country by driving around looking for stock in the early days and delivering them to customers later; meeting people from nearly every county and from all walks of life; searching for suitable means of transportation for these animals by air, on trains, by boat and road; finding or constructing suitable vehicles for them such as carts, traps and donkey-sized trailers, the latter never before made over here; studying the dietary and medicinal requirements of donkeys as distinct from horses; learning about local husbandry, the use and avoidance of certain manures on our land.

We discovered how to build shelters suitable for both winter and summer use and also mobile ones for removal from leased land; how to arrange the stud-life for mares at home and for visiting mares; also acting as nurse, midwife and nannie. Then there was the never ending contact with the blacksmith, as excessive dampness makes donkeys' hooves, more pliable than those of horses, grow faster; and the intermittent business with vets, agricultural advisers, local authority officials and many others. Later when our stud opened to the public and became a tourist attraction, we met reporters, VIPs, photographers, television teams and visitors from many lands, one and all interested in or working with donkeys.

All this was a long way from those early days when we decided to buy our first mares. Almost simultaneously, although coming from different homes, the two new donkey ladies converged at their destination. Entering the paddock they gave each other the once-over look, exchanged a few sniffs, munched a few mouthfuls of grass as though to fortify themselves for the ordeal to come, then treaded their way daintily, if a little hesitantly, to meet us at the railings. The encounter was, like all important first meetings should be, brief, warm but with a promise of things to come.

I doubt if two young asses ever before experienced such halcyon days as did these first arrivals to Medina House. If they had been the world's most valuable bloodstock no better treatment would have ensued. They were VIPs to us and, if the love affair was a little one-sided to start with, our subsequent treacherous behaviour more than balanced the matter, for very soon their sovereignty was violated as more mares began to arrive on the scene. So pleased were we with our new family that we soon felt obliged to purchase more. When these were introduced into the paddock, the original occupants showed the little green eye of jealousy, and we experienced no little difficulty in getting acquainted with the new girls, what with the pushings and shovings that went on by the first pair in an effort to keep the others in what was considered their proper place – as far away from us as possible! Great diplomacy was required for a while as yet more mares arrived, and only when extra land was purchased were relationships easier to handle. Donkeys make their special chums when many are herded together and, having noticed this trait, we always do our best to respect it and keep friends in the same field.

Warming to our new interest daily, in spite of the somewhat bewildered enquiries from neighbours as to what we were going to do 'with all them asses', we made what turned out to be a decision of resounding importance – we acquired a stallion. That we were now a donkey stud was beyond dispute, but that we all lived happily, quietly and peacefully ever after is another matter!

It was a fine day when himself 'landed', to use the local expression for arrivals of any kind. Straightaway the stallion announced his presence with a bray that reverberated from one end of the parish to the other. One and all got the message, though it was received with somewhat mixed reactions. The brides-to-be, idly passing the time away grazing or dozing in the sun, lifted their heads in unison, remained frozen for seconds in unbelieving surprise, until an encore dispelled their doubts, then their answering cries of welcome varied in tone. From those mares ready for married bliss, the brays came across louder and more frequently, followed by a rhythmic opening and shutting of the mouth, a sign, as we soon learnt, that they were ready and anxious for mating. The other mares, having politely acknowledged the arrival of their lord and master – no women's lib here – resumed their normal activities.

At first the stallion was put in a nearby field on his own, obviously this did not suit at all, as he galloped madly around, emitting powerful brays of indignation and glaring at the encircling walls which prevented him from joining his lady-loves. Having been previously informed that donkey stallions would think nothing of attempting Becher's Brook when in amorous pursuit, we decided that a hasty marriage was the only answer. One of the 'in-season' mares, ready for mating, was led into a stable, then the stallion was introduced. Afterwards they were put in a field together and carried on with the 'honeymoon'. We find it best not to mate mares until they are three or four years old. As other mares which we wished to mate came in season the same procedure was repeated, and the stallion settled down happily in the company of his harem.

All matrimonial plans were not so successfully organised however. As the gestation period for a donkey is on average a year and five days, though it can range from eleven to fourteen months, we try and arrange the mating mostly in late spring, for summer foaling the next year. Yet, in spite of careful vigilance, itinerant donkey stallions paid us unofficial visits from time to time, and our own sires also broke out from their paddocks on occasions to mate with those other than their intended spouses, too often putting paid to my preconceived breeding plans. Thus the herd gradually became larger than I had remotely envisaged.

Most stallions are gay Lotharios and ours are no exception; two especially will take off in amorous search at any opportunity. Having scoured the countryside in search of them one autumn and made umpteen enquiries as to their whereabouts, a local wit told us 'sure they've gone on to Lisdoonvarna for a wife'. By repute, the farmers come to this local town on their holidays, after the harvest is in, looking for wives. And sure enough it was on the road ahead that our strays were found!

From amongst the first lot of mares bought, two, Rainbow and Betty Peg, were in foal. Rainbow was so called because we first saw her in a coastal field framed by a perfect rainbow. Betty Peg's somewhat strange name sprang from my superstitious dislike of change: the day I bought the mare from an elderly farmer he called her Betty, but when I collected her, he called her Peg. By the time I realised the discrepancy I was homeward bound with – Betty Peg! A few months later two colts were born. Rainbow had a brown lad – Raindrop, her first foal which arrived early one June evening after a normal delivery time of half an hour. And two weeks later Betty Peg's little black boy made a quartet in the front paddock.

When we first put a mare in the paddock with her new foal to join the others, the dam always guides it forward by nudging each quarter alternatively with her head, which she swings from side to side, exerting the pressure where necessary to shove the foal to the desired place, in a corner or by a fence, where she can graze between it and any possible violator of their privacy. Should the others show more than a polite interest at their arrival, she shoves the little one forward with alacrity, sometimes lifting its hind legs high off the ground in her haste while swerving her own quarters around in a menacing manner towards the advancing party. If the curious newcomer is another foal, she turns around and makes a rush at it to shoo it away, but will not kick out at it or hurt it in any way, as she might its mother.

The newcomer's wish for privacy is generally respected for a day or so, then the foals begin making overtures to each other. This is a most entertaining affair. The foals will start staring at each other for a while, one perhaps walking a little towards the other one. Suddenly the baby will begin to canter around its dam as fast as it can on its still rather wobbly legs, bravely taking increasingly wider circles out into the world, even veering towards the other foal which it knows is watching, until quite exhausted it pulls up triumphantly alongside the mare and turns towards the other foal as though to say 'look what I can do'! Its triumph is short-lived. The older one, not to be outdone by this newcomer, starts a marathon show-off, galloping around the paddock at astonishingly high speed, a really alarming procedure to those witnessing it for the first time. Round and round it goes, slowing occasionally to give a buck and a fierce little kick out at nothing in particular, then off again at full speed for ages until, in an act of supreme bravery, it makes a dash for it and passes around the new mother and foal and ends up proudly beside its own parent. Duly impressed by all this, the younger foal now has a little thinking to do and, deciding this would be better done while taking refreshment, goes to it, while the undisputed winner of the display feels he has earned the meal which he too proceeds to devour.

Although the respective mothers are grazing away quietly, let it not be thought that they are oblivious to what is going on. Outwardly calm but inwardly alert they are wise to every move. The foals, seemingly less uppity after a satisfying repast, make their way tentatively towards each other and, after exchanging nose to nose greetings, decide to be friends. When there are a number of older foals in the paddock, these overtures may be started by two or more of them giving a combined display of speed and antics in order to encourage the new member to test his skill and stamina.

Accidents occasionally occur in these romps, especially in our front paddock which is on a slope. A young racer, meeting an unexpected level of ground at high speed can do a spectacular somersault, or an equally spectacular 'rear end skid' when, unable to make a sudden stop, the hind legs shoot between the forelegs bringing the tail end abruptly to the ground, resulting in a decidedly undignified skid on the rear end along the grass, before all extremities are unravelled and an upright posture resumed! Surprisingly, not much damage is done by such acrobatics, although we had a nasty experience once when a galloping foal shot out one of those excited kicks at nothing and unintentionally hit another, younger animal on the forehead, knocking it out for the count. A hasty call to the vet was necessary to resuscitate the casualty. Another speedy youngster, knowing that he had an appreciative audience, went on and on playing to the gallery for so long that he didn't know whether he was coming or going and landed up for refuelling beside the wrong mother, until an indignant snort sent him staggering back to the home front.

We were lucky in that our first few donkeys were friendly creatures, with the one exception, a young mare who before we bought her was in foal as a yearling, and then lost the foal in sad circumstances when she was just a two-year-old. We have owned her now for ten years and it took from four to five years before we overcame her nervousness and won her confidence. She still views strangers, even when accompanied by one of us, with suspicion. Despite her early upset, I feel that her nervous disposition may also have been hereditary.

An interesting feature of this mare's behaviour is that she invariably foals standing up, a trait she has passed on to the first of her stock born here. She is never overly temperamental with the arrival of her foals, just nervously elusive, which makes it difficult to become friends with the new foals in their infancy, as she whisks them away before one can get near them. As time goes on the tension eases, but her foals are not as entertaining as the ones allowed to develop their own rapport with us from birth.

This mare's firstborn, called Nickel, became the inseparable companion of Cledagh, a filly born at the same time. The two came into season at a similar period and were mated. As their foaling time came around they were still together. Cledagh produced a broken-coloured (skewbald) colt, which settled down happily with Mum and 'Auntie' Nickel in attendance. The *menage à trois* was not destined to last for long as the next day, a Sunday morning when my helpers and all my neighbours were at church, Nickel decided to foal, like her mother, standing up. Things were not going too easily with her and, even though she is a quiet and gentle creature, it was no simple matter for one person to give her the assistance she required, as her refusal to lie down necessitated someone to hold her and another to aid the birth. As already stated, a normal birth takes approximately half an hour, but sometimes a little longer for a first-foaling mare. Nickel was a first foaler, but it was long over the half hour since she started walking agitatedly around the paddock in labour, with only a little visible result for her pains. I telephoned our vets but both were out. There was nothing else for it, I must enter the arena alone. Coming over the crest of the hill on her return home, one of my assistants was astonished to see in the distance my head darting to and fro above the wall. She was even more astonished when she got closer and saw a frantic 'midwife' sidling from one end of the still-expectant mare to the other in an effort to get her to 'stand and deliver'. Quickly she came to my aid and together we helped the mare bring forth the goods in the form of a lovely white and dark-brown colt foal. She gave birth still standing up and shortly afterwards went off to join the others, leaving her hard-fought-for prize by itself! We brought her back to the foal which she allowed to suckle; but showed little interest in it and, as soon as our backs were turned, off she went to rejoin her chums.

It was a strong foal, steady on its legs, and it had fed and already passed its first droppings. As the day was warm and sunny we thought to leave all four alone now and watch the result from a distance. The new arrival tottered about for a while with those little jerky movements so typical of the newly born donkey foal. He veered in all directions, then looked around forlornly before those little legs, which in all foals never cease to amaze us by the length of time they can stay upright after their first uprising, crumpled up and deposited a lonely looking little bundle of white and brown fluff sleepily among the meadow flowers.

The other three remained together until, passing within sight of the sleeping foal, they idly poked their noses at the little one and meandered off again, leaving it looking perplexedly and drowsily after them.

As time went on and the mare did not return, we again intervened, reintroducing mother and son at a suitable point for the latter to take milk, leaving them alone while the meal was in progress and hoping that they would now remain together. But alas, once 'tea' was over, the mare departed to join her friends at the other end of the field. At periodic intervals we attempted reintroductions without success and, as evening approached and there were rain clouds in sight, we realised this situation must not be allowed to continue. As Mum showed little instinctive knowledge of 'aftercare', we took the matter in hand ourselves. If the weather had not been fine, we would have taken action much sooner. In normal circumstances a mare will pay attention to her foal after the birth, not only helping it out of its foetal membrane but also licking it constantly to dry and warm it and encourage its circulation. Such action was not necessary in this case because of the balmy weather.

We put the mare and foal in a stable by themselves and sprinkled a little salt on the foal's back, an inducement to equine mothers to lick and pay attention to their offspring. After a few plaintive hee-haws over the half-door of the stable the mare, receiving no response save a reproachful look from her son, shuffled around the stable until, greatly to her surprise so it seemed, she discovered her disconsolate foal. Approaching him, as though for the first time, she commenced to spring-clean him thoroughly, no place escaped as he was licked up as far as possible and down as far as possible, then almost exhausted, though blissfully happy, he was manoeuvred into position to partake of supper. Greatly relieved by these activities we too retired to our supper, and to learn that there were other important things taking place in the world – for it was Sunday, 20 July 1969, the day of man's first landing on the moon.

Next day all seemed well with both Nickel and her foal, by now named Money Moon but, deciding to take no chances, we put them in a field by themselves. They settled down together and a few days later rejoined the others without further upset. There could have been tiresome and worrying days ahead for us should the mare wittingly or unwittingly have deprived the foal of its milk or should the foal have been unable to obtain it for itself. This latter difficulty cropped up with a friend of mine when her newly born foal would not, or could not, suck from its dam. I quote from what she wrote to me:

> Still the foal did not suck; even getting the teat into her mouth she simply would not suck. I milked the dam and fed a few teaspoonfuls to the foal. She swallowed with relish, but simply seemed not to know how to suck. I fed her on her mother's milk every two hours, but the next day after several more attempts to get her to suck normally, I tried her with a bottle and teat. It took me a full day to make her suck the teat, always with the mother's milk in the bottle. Now, I thought it is plain sailing but no, still she would not suck from her dam, who was by this time decidedly crusty about letting the foal near her business end. Also the milk was drying up, due to my drawing off far more than nature intended every two hours.

Hurriedly procuring substitute feeding available for horse and pony foals, and gauging the amount suitable for donkey foals, this devoted foster mother bottle-fed from May to September!

> At first I fed the foal every two hours but, after the first week, I cut it down to every four. The mare did not object at all. I always brought a tit-bit for herself and she was full of protective instinct in every way, except in giving suck to her baby. As time went on we progressed from beer bottle to half gin bottle to whisky bottle and a half vodka bottle. In September she went on to the 'hard stuff', ie foal pellets mixed with flaked maize and a dash of Ribena and sugar. It is Christmas time now and she is almost as big as her mother.

A credit to you, Madam, say I.

Last year we took in a ten-day-old orphan foal which had lost its dam at birth and had been hand-fed ever since, but unfortunately not often enough. The owners who have business premises in a country town looked after it there in the yard and stable from 8am to 11pm, where it was well-fed and petted affectionately by everyone. Having no place in which to keep the donkey at their home, it was housed alone at their business premises the remaining nine night-time hours without nourishment, maternal warmth or companionship. When we came on the scene, we were told that it had been ailing for the past few days, also that the vet had seen it that morning and gave little hope of its survival. The gap during the long night hours without sustenance had been too much for the general well-being of such a young creature and the excellent care it received during the day wasn't sufficient to offset the extra care he needed during the long lonely nights. For three days and nights we nursed the dear wee creature here, but all to no avail as he never rallied. It was sad news for the owners on their next daily visit and it was sad news for us too as we had grown so fond of this plucky little fellow in those few days; he seemed to know that we were trying to help him and we felt that he was making every effort to recover, but he just did not have sufficient strength. He was one of God's small creatures we shall always remember.

As with humans, very young animals require feeding little and often and will seldom thrive or even survive without the warmth of maternal care or constant companionship. The ideal answer to an orphaned donkey-foal is a willing donkey foster mother but, as this is seldom available, here are a few points for the owner foster mother to bear in mind. Feed the foal every few hours at first on a suitable substitute milk – goat's milk being a first choice – any baby foods, cow's milk diluted or, more economically, the pony and horse foal milk substitutes. Also try to use a teat that resembles its mother's, such as those used with lambs, and only make a small hole in it, so that the foal can suck soothingly over a reasonable period, as nature intended. If the hole is too large the foal will gulp down the milk, perhaps sensing the feeder's possible wish to get the job over quickly, and thereby building up tension. This will do little to help the donkey digest its food, food that is unnatural to it anyway and given by a parent that is likewise! The act of sucking has a soothing effect in itself. Give the new arrival an affectionate mare donkey as a companion who will give it warming attentions, or any other accommodating animal. If these are not available then bring it near to hand, so that it can at least hear life going on around it and to make it easier for you to pay it as much attention as possible until it has got a firm hold on life.

Since I last wrote a book about donkeys, some eight years ago, new information has come my way on coping with certain matters, particularly breeding, and I feel these facts are worth mentioning here, even if they do read rather like a laundry list! We now find it best not to mate the mares for the first time until they are three or four years old. We also keep our foals with their dams for at least a year and let this same period pass without getting the mare in foal again. Incidentally, we inoculate all our animals against tetanus (lock-jaw). When a mare with foal at foot comes into season, any time from about six or seven days after giving birth, the foal is liable to suffer from diarrhoea, known as scouring. While this does not necessarily indicate that the foal is ill, it is well worthwhile keeping a special eye on it then to see that the scours stop when the mare comes 'off season'. It is most important to prevent dehydration of foals that are scouring constantly and I find warm water with glucose is most helpful here. Scouring is not a disease in itself, only a symptom that might lead to more serious trouble if not watched, so it is advisable to contact your vet should a foal continue to scour for more than forty-eight hours when its dam is not in season.

Research work carried out by the Animal Health Trust has persuaded them that the umbilical cord of a newborn foal requires no human attention whatsoever after a normal birth. It should be left alone to break at the correct place and time (generally by the movement of the mare), and not be cut by scissors. Too early severance can cause the foal a loss of placental foetal blood which, a recent report suggests, is no good thing: 'apart from the possibility that specific illnesses might sometimes be precipitated by this blood loss, the general interests of the animal are better served when they are allowed to regain this blood.' Cutting the cord could allow bacteria to enter through the navel, and administering strong antiseptic to prevent this can damage any tissues with which it comes in contact.

Infrequently foals are born in a state of suspended animation (without movement and seemingly without life). Energetic measures are then immediately required to stimulate respiration. Lifting the foal up by the hind legs so that mucus or saliva can pass out from the respiratory passages, massaging the body with rough cloths and slapping it should be carried out before life is despaired of.

Some foals make a practice of eating droppings (faeces). While this is a most unattractive habit, I have not known it do them any harm.

In our early days we never kept stallions together but, as our herd increased in size, we found it expedient to do so and have had as many as thirteen stallions in a large field. In the winter months all is well, but during the times when a mare is anywhere in the vicinity there are plenty of high-jinks, and a wealth of reproachful hee-haws fill the air, though nothing worse than a nip or two occurs! I do not think we could keep so many together in a hot climate or when 'feeling their oats'.

Despite all such information and the growing expertise born of experience, our donkeys still continue to surprise us. One day, for instance, after examination of some heavily in-foal mares in the paddock, it was decided, as the weather forecast threatened rain, to bring one of them, Sisi, into the yard for the night as she looked like foaling before another day dawned. Her pal, Ras Shamra, who did not appear to be near foaling just yet, was to come in with Sisi for company as we never take one singly from a group, except in special circumstances.

Sure enough, during the night watch, Sisi foaled under the shed in the yard without any trouble, and without any rain either, though the sky still looked threatening in the early morning light. The foal was a beauty, just the sex and colour we had hoped for and as saucy as you please. In fact, it was so frisky that we feared to leave it loose around the yard for the remainder of the night and decided to put both mare and foal in the stable. This was our usual routine under such weather conditions and suited the mare and foal admirably – but not so Ras! Until then she had been standing quietly by munching hay and minding her own business, as is generally the case with the non-active companions on such occasions, but the minute after we had closed the stable, she became highly indignant. Putting her head over the door Ras let the occupants know her objections at being left out on her own. She then came over to us and complained while we were busy tidying up. Then, getting little attention from any direction, she let out a protest that was far too noisy for that time of night, so to try and circumvent any further eruptions we shoved her face into a bowl of oats and told her to mind her manners before we went off to roost.

Waking earlier than usual after these nocturnal activities I found that the rain had given us a miss, so decided to go outside and transfer the youngest member of our fraternity from stable to paddock. Imagine my utter bewilderment to discover another even younger member quietly taking his breakfast. A now sedate and complacent-looking Ras, seemingly provoked by our churlish treatment in removing her company, had produced her own company – and that was that. It was a truly remarkable exploit, as I had examined her the evening before when she had shown none of the physical signs of an imminent birth and, except for her carry-on of a few hours earlier, her behaviour showed none either. Seldom has one of these surprising animals surprised me more!

No unusual troubles with those births, nevertheless another mare, Turf, managed to get herself into a tight corner. Late one evening we saw that she had started to foal and, keeping an eye on her from an upstairs window, we saw she remained an inordinately long time lying down in one corner of the field and obviously in labour. Noel, our assistant and I decided we had better investigate and it was lucky that we did, for we found her 'busy end' was too close to the large stone slabs that formed the boundary of the field and thus, while the mare made every effort to eject the foal, the slabs prevented its entry into the world. We dragged the mare's hind quarters away from the corner and hey presto another baby ass was born. This was a mare who had foaled many times before without mishap and the incident showed once again how necessary it is to take nothing for granted in the foaling season; though it is not always easy to be in the right place at the right time when there are many things requiring attention.

Are donkeys deliberately provoking? I would rather not answer that, but merely cite a few examples of their behaviour. You put your donkey in a large grassy field, not knowing that somewhere in that fine pasture lurks a tin can open at both ends. Do not worry, your donkey is bound to find it for you, and soon you will be trying to cut an offending 'bracelet' off a tender limb, wondering why the tin opener is not geared for such emergencies. You have recently sold one of the herd and for the last few days have been busy titivating it for the new owner. On the day of departure, guess whose tail has been chewed to pieces? Your mare has foaled successfully, but the night is turning wet so mother and baby are put in the stable. Someone has removed the water bucket and all you can find to replace it is a large oval plastic basin. That will do nicely for the time being you think and, returning for a last peep after your cuppa, you find the foal fits into it perfectly, and what is left of the water too! Who would have visualised such a cradle?

One such event which I often remember with astonishment took place in the early hours of the morning. Waiting for a first-foaling mare to do her job, our night watchers, weary after recent spells on duty, welcomed a kind suggestion from my daughter, who had just come home from abroad, that she would replace them and share the vigil with me. The donkey was enclosed in our fairly large yard, and the open shed under which the mares usually foaled was visible from certain of the house windows. At scheduled intervals during the night we both peeped out and all seemed well until, at my second last rising, I delayed awhile as the mare appeared restless; but as she seemed to settle down so did I. After a short while I had another look and, seeing her standing quietly alone, I returned wearily to bed. My head was hardly on the pillow before my daughter came bounding into the room to say she thought the mare had foaled. She too had seen the mare standing alone but, hearing a rustling in the straw at the other end of the shed, she had gone outside to investigate and seen something moving there. Knowing that the straw was stacked a good distance away from the mare with slats of wood and a window-frame laid against it, I gave her little credence but, feeling that such conscientious solicitude warranted some response, I reeled back into action and followed her to the yard. As the torch's rays glided over the mound of straw, a rustle came from the farthest corner and the light picked out a tiny pair of black wobbly ears. Clambering over the straw we found the still wet foal in the corner of the shed at least twenty-five feet away from its dam. How it got through the wooden laths and the window-frame, and along between about fifteen feet of straw and the wall without injury, I shall never know, as it could not have clambered over the mound of straw – or could it?

Then again, against our better judgement we purchased Irish Lace, a pretty young mare with a large growth of warts on the side of her udder, because she looked so sad and lonely. The vets warned that any effort to remove the warts could injure the mammary glands and that any foal she might have must do the best it could with one teat and hand-feeding. Ever hopeful, we examined the warts every now and again for about two years but there was no change. So, with Irish Lace's permission we decided to marry her. About halfway through her pregnancy, when introducing her to a new assistant as the mare with the growth of warts and whose foal would need special care, we found there was absolutely no sign of a wart anywhere; only signs of utter amazement from me and a smug look from Lacy!

Rainbow, mentioned earlier, now a young matron who has produced her share of foals, enjoys wiling away a fine afternoon giving rides in the paddock. But, when she feels that she has done more than her share, she makes straight for a low-roofed shelter which she knows she could enter alone, leaving her rider clinging to the roof, if we did not take the precaution of latching the door.

This same mare was instrumental in teaching me an important lesson – never for a second lay impediments on a stable floor. One day while changing haybags I stupidly put the empty bag on the floor while tying up the full one. Rainbow, never a laggard where her appetite is concerned, stepped forward hurriedly and her legs became tangled in the network. In an effort to free them she got even more entwined and scared too. This was where our friendship stood the test as, clasping her head, I held it firmly by one hand and, while talking soothingly, my other hand caressed her until it gradually sidled down to free first one then the other foreleg and, mercifully at last, the only hind leg involved. I had learned my lesson the hard way, but it would undoubtedly have been a harder one had we not been good friends.

Sometimes one feels the lesson is unmerited and the outcome undeserved, as with the death of our handsome chestnut stallion Ard-Ri. He was wintering on the farm of some kind friends in the midlands, together with his gelding companion. After some cattle had mysteriously got out of the same roadside field in which they were all grazing, our friends kindly moved the donkeys to the field in front of their house for extra surveillance. Little did they think that the swing, which gave so much pleasure to the children, could prove lethal to a donkey, until to their great dismay they found Ard-Ri hanging from it. It is only since this happened that I have heard of similar cases with ponies as victims.

Another distressing incident, though not a fatal one, took place some years ago. Not there at the time it happened, I still feel perplexed that the final outcome was not prevented. Cledagh, a quiet, young mare which we had bred ourselves, and which was in season, was being removed from her field to be mated elsewhere. As she was being loaded into the trailer, the hoof from a hind leg was caught in the opening between the back door and the trailer and taken completely off. She suffered greatly for some time and it was four weeks before she left her stable, though in about eight or nine months' time she had grown a new hoof.

I later saw this same mare do a very strange thing when her weeks-old foal caught a severe chill and both had to be stabled. In such emergencies we keep a constant vigil, as sick donkeys are not good fighters and so we give them plenty of attention to encourage recovery. As the foal was taking little food, we had been milking the mare periodically. During the night Cledagh became fidgety and uncomfortable and I realised she needed milking again, but delayed for fear of disturbing the sleeping foal. The mare had no such qualms and, lifting a hind leg she plunged her head towards her udder repeatedly, with her mouth open. From what I could see in the dim light, and as I deduced by her relaxed air afterwards, she had not waited for anyone's convenience, but had milked herself sufficiently to give relief.

Betty Peg, known to us as the Houdini of donkeys, never remains in one place for long and cares not who knows of her escapist tricks. She is a shameless hussy who spends her life 'loitering with intent' or 'breaking and entering', even committing 'grand larceny'. Her case history is a lurid one, recording the use of 'leg cuffs' and the fear that she will be 'on probation' for life. The latest report on her conduct arrived today from friends at Rivioli Cottage, Ennistymon, on whose land she is grazing: 'Betty Peg got out under the wire, went to visit the Drooney farm, found a bag of chick mash, undid the tie and helped herself. You ought to put her on the stage, she would make a fortune! Fortunately the Drooneys enjoyed it too, as they saw her performance.' In between her escapades Betty Peg has presented us with some delightful foals and, in spite of the fact that stable doors have been kicked to pieces when some incarceration has been absolutely necessary, she will serve a life sentence here with us.

We have learned to adapt to Betty Peg's foibles, but all too often harassed or unthinking people fail to understand their

Plate 1 The author with the brown mare Turf and her colt foal Rick whose unusual birth is described in chapter 2 *(The Word)*

Plate 2 Truly asses galore at the Spanish Point stud *(The Word)*

Plate 3 A working donkey collecting seaweed on the Clare coast

Plate 4 This donkey too is employed in the traditional manner with panniers in which to carry peat from the bogs

animals' characters and blame the poor creatures for man's own lack of understanding. For instance, a mare heavily in season may be mistakenly put in a field too near a rampant stallion with the result that he breaks out causing general chaos and possible injury to himself in the process. Or an in-foal mare, especially a maiden one, may be left unattended when due to foal, losing her offspring because human assistance was not available when needed. Thus, while we rush around bemoaning our lot and perhaps for a fleeting second wish these troublesome animals to a donkey's Hades, we forget that it was not they, but human carelessness, which caused our exasperation.

3   On the Menu

If you were to ask McCann's ass, whom one meets on many a page of James Stephens's book *The Demi-Gods*, his thoughts on a donkey's diet, you would be unlikely to get an answer in a nutshell. Carrots he views from many an angle, covering their shape, colour, the way they look in a bucket, and the crunching noise they make when bitten. Eventually, after many other thoughts concerning them, he comes to the conclusion that all carrots taste alike and are simply a 'companionable food'. Thistles, he recalls, make a 'swishing noise', whereas 'grass does not make any noise at all; it slips dumbly to the sepulchre, and makes no sign. Bread makes no sound either when it is eaten by an ass; it has an interesting taste, and it clings about one's teeth for a long time.' As for apples, they have 'a good smell and a joyful crunch, but the taste of sugar lasts longer than anything else; it has a short sharp crunch that is like a curse, and instantly it blesses you with the taste of it'.

He meditates on hay which can be eaten in large mouthfuls: 'it has a chip and a crack at the first bite, and then it says no more'. It is also 'a friendly food and very good for the hungry'.

As for oats: 'they are a debauch; they make you proud, so that you want to kick the front out of a cart, and climb a tree, and bite a cow and chase chickens'. Thinking nice thoughts like these helped McCann's ass forget how wet and uncomfortable he was, but it is doubtful if all donkeys have such colourful thoughts when wet and hungry and, even if they had, they could not subsist on them for long.

A suitable diet for donkeys is always a matter for discussion among owners, particularly those who have large numbers of the animals and live in regions where the climatic changes are at variance with those weather conditions in which donkeys have been observed to thrive. Less than half a century ago grazing for equines was not hard to come by here, and good grazing it was too in most places, contributing much to the success of Irish bloodstock around the world. The ass had his fair share of the green pastures and, as he is content with more roughage than is the horse, there was always a bite for him in the summertime, even if his owners, less affluent than horse owners, cut him down on the winter's bite of hay. Looking back, it seems that in those days there were so many acres per animal, and nowadays so many animals per acre.

Nearly all the vicissitudes we have experienced with our donkeys, especially with the foals, can be put down to difficulties in coping adequately with the effects of both climate and diet on them. As the latter depends to a great extent on the former, we return again to the donkey's greatest adversary in this scenic outpost of western Europe, the changeable climatic conditions. That the animal has survived here over the last few centuries is apparent but, if the information I have gleaned talking to country folk up and down the west coast is correct, and also my own observations, then the percentage of survival cannot be very high. Many people will state that the ass's continuing here in Ireland must mean that it is a hardy animal, but I cannot accept this. It may have *survived*, but there has always been a high mortality rate among very young foals, especially if they are born in excessively wet weather and are left uncared for. In the early weeks their fluffy baby coat is not as rain repellent as it will become later and, if foals are subjected to repeated drenchings they catch a chill which, if not attended to immediately, too often turns into pneumonia and proves fatal. Equally, if the babies are born when excessively hot weather during the day is followed by unusually cold nights, as has happened here, the same chill will result as the little ones get overheated as they lie in the sun, then the quick change in temperature lowers their resistance to colds. The white and broken-coloured foals fall victim to these quick-changing weather extremes more often than the darker ones. Without a doubt, shelter of some sort, preferably an open one in a field, is of utmost importance to the well-being of these animals whose ancestors mostly came from dry and arid climates.

Exactly how and when the ass first came to Ireland is not known, though he has been traced back as far as the middle of the seventeenth century, so we do not know what the first of his ancestors over here looked like physically. We do know that around the end of the eighteenth and the beginning of the nineteenth century some large Spanish male asses were brought to this country to breed mules. Mr Dubourdieu, in his volume on Londonderry, tells us that some years earlier than 1812 a Mr McNeill imported an ass from Malaga, Spain, for this purpose and was very successful. He describes the animal as above 14 hands high, 'his head not of that heavy, dull cast so common in our unfortunate creatures of the same species'. Earlier still, in 1753, the Royal Dublin Society offered a reward of £20 for the importation of a Spanish ass to breed mules, and much later, from 1891–1923, the Congested District Board (with which, incidentally, my grandfather was associated), had plans to bring in larger asses to improve the breed for working purposes. Unless these male asses were laggards at love in a cold climate, they must have sired a share of large offspring. How strange then that merely a few decades later the very large ass is already a rarity in this country.

I used often to be asked, mostly by older people, if I knew which counties were reputed in the past to have had the best asses. Should I plead ignorance, the answer was invariably the same –

Kerry and Roscommon. Knowing that the best ass nearly always means the *largest* animal to the country folk who for years have used them solely for labour, this reply has some significance. In these counties, or most parts of them, the climate is the most agreeable for donkeys. Kerry, in the extreme south-west, is well known to have a mild climate throughout the year and its long mountain ranges give shelter from the Atlantic storms. Roscommon, in the west midlands, is mostly rather high above sea level and has a county between it and the Atlantic and a fair share of hills for added shelter. On average these two counties seem to have provided greater shelter and warmth for their donkey population than did the others, and it is for that reason I feel that the large donkeys survived there longer than in any other parts of Ireland.

In our stud, we breed mostly the middle-sized animal, ranging from 38 to 42in in height, with the odd one under or over those figures, but five or six years ago I bought a grey/brown stallion from Roscommon of around 45in called Tommyduffy. He was supposed to be one of a twin, and also to have produced varied coloured and interesting looking stock. A young mare sired by him belonged to a friend of ours, and looked so like one of the Asiatic wild asses, the onager, that when we heard Tommyduffy was for sale, we decided to make a bid for him. Never shall I forget the day I went to collect him. Having more or less settled the deal by letter, an unusual proceeding over here, I set off with the trailer to fetch the donkey.

It was over a three-hour journey before I located his owner's home way up on the side of a hill, and my reception was one of the strangest I have ever received – nearly all the family were in floods of tears! A little dismayed by this and in spite of the warm welcome given to me, I refused the refreshments so kindly offered, excusing myself on the grounds of my haste to start on the long journey home. Two of the children were then dispatched up the hillside to fetch Tommyduffy and, as the tearful sobs which had dwindled down to sniffles for a while were renewed by the remaining children, I was told the cause. It seems they were unable to get any place nearby in which to keep the donkey, and he would not in future be permitted to roam the hillside around them, where he had been for the last ten years, ever since he had come to them as a weanling when the owners were first married. The children who had known him all their lives were devoted to him, as were the parents, and all were loath to part with him. Feeling like a thief and almost as upset as they were, I quickly helped load Tommyduffy into the trailer and set off for home, with the promise to write and tell them how he fared in his new abode; a promise that I kept gladly, for I had met few vendors with such a real affection for their pet.

Although we paid Tommyduffy a lot of attention, giving him company, and he responded with his habitual gentleness to both man and beast, he was, nevertheless, a 'loner'. We are sure he missed his family and his fancy-free days on the sheltered hillside in Roscommon. He spent more time than any of the other donkeys in his open shelter and during his first winter with us he got rheumatism. Not so bad at first, it then increased so rapidly that to save him undue suffering during the very bad winter of 1972-3 we had him put to sleep. Perhaps this is just a singular instance and I am over-careful, but I would now think twice before bringing an aged ass from a region he has been brought up in to a place where living conditions were less suitable to his species. On the large hillside he had roamed through for ten years he had an abundant selection of the coarse herbage favoured by donkeys, and avoided the rigours of the weather conditions experienced on our coast. Incidentally the few mares he served produced fine foals, our working mare Shubad being by him.

Whenever there is mention of the ass and its diet by writers on the history of animals or in encyclopedias of agriculture, compendiums of veterinary science, zoological lore and other such studious writings of up to fifty years ago, there are nearly always allusions to this same 'coarse herbage'. As Thomas Brown, MPS, wrote in his *Compendium of Veterinary Science and Practice* (1904): 'His temperance is very great, being able to subsist on a scanty meal of the coarsest herbage.' In an article

'Irish Zoology No 11' from the *Irish Penny Magazine*, 1833, the opinion was that '... any weed or thistle contents him, but he is said to show preference for the narrow-leaved plantain, (*Plantago lanceolata*) above every other herb in the pasturage'. Even earlier, M de Buffon (1707-88), wrote of the donkey's contenting himself with the most harsh and disagreeable herbs, which other animals will scarcely touch. And, according to the Abbe la Pluche: 'He is very serviceable to many persons who are not able to buy or keep horses; especially where they live near heaths or commons, the barrenest of which will keep him; being contented with any kind of coarse herbage such as dry leaves, stalks, thistles, briars, chaff and any sort of straw.' And a late discovery, for us anyway, is the donkey's love of nettle roots as opposed to the plant.

I wish we had known more about this taste for roughage when we first reseeded our pastures. Although we had often heard it said that donkeys would eat any old thing we were inclined to think that such a selection was one of necessity not of choice and so, wishing to give them what we thought was the best grazing, we sowed too rich a herbage. This misjudgement helped to cause us much trouble and sorrow before too long.

The winter of 1968-9 was a long one due to a late spring. The east wind, which generally visits us in early March, remained around longer than usual, and the ground was too wet and cold for there to be the normal spring growth. The front paddock and nearby fields had become rather skinned during the remarkably dry and warm summer of the previous year so, as April dawned with little sign of growth, we decided to put down some quick-action artificial manure in these places. Artificial manures had not been used much in our particular area to date and, although we have kept a Donkey Diary since 1965, we only included husbandry notes after 1969, so that we do not know for certain whether or not we had ever used chemical manure of any kind on the land previously. Anxious to provide adequate grazing for the new season's foals we had possibly used some artificial form of fertiliser the previous autumn. Cattle manure for sale is not very plentiful locally and it would have taken more labour than we had at the time to fetch and spread it.

Aware that there would not, in any case, be much grass around by the time the first few of our twenty-two foaling mares produced their young in March and April, we had been giving these mares extra care over the winter. All went well with the first foals which were born from the beginning of March until about the end of May when, at last, and much to our relief, there was a perceptible growth of rich green grass. We all looked forward to an easing of hand-feeding work, but little did we guess at the horrors which the next five or six weeks had in store for us.

On 1 June, one of the foals born in mid-May suffered from the form of acute diarrhoea described previously as scouring. This we treated as we had treated other foals in the past which might have caught a slight chill or any other infection. When the youngster did not respond, we called in the vet to treat it professionally, but all to no avail, it continued scouring and died a few days later. We did not have an autopsy as we were exceptionally busy and thought that perhaps we had not attended early enough to this foal's complaint, or called in the vet too late when the foal was too weak to respond to treatment. Soon more foals were arriving and others were becoming ill. The symptoms were always the same, a drawing up of their little legs in a sort of clenching movement (called by us the 'discomfort dance'), while standing listlessly around emitting a thin watery scour from time to time, mostly after a feed. They also frequently became lame in one, and sometimes two, of their legs. Only the second batch of foals were affected, not the early ones born in March and April, which fortunately were in fine fettle.

As more and more foals were smitten with this same malady we became frantic with worry as there did not seem to be any obvious cause or cure. We stabled the ones which were in the worst shape so that we could observe them more closely and, at the same time, we put the mares out in the fields every now and again to graze, so that they would not lose their milk, and the foals continued to feed until they lost the strength to do so. The next foal to die, an eight-day-old colt, had a more terrible and different ending than the others; for some time before he expired he threw himself around the stable in agony and we could only look on helpless. An autopsy later, in Dublin, showed that his death was due to an intussusception, caused by a portion of the bowel telescoping into the portion below it, with resulting intense pain. Such a terrible affliction can be brought on by continual scouring. The autopsy also showed that the lining of the stomach was perforated with little holes (ulcers). Another foal, just three weeks old, died the next day and its body also was sent to Dublin.

Three days later, and before we had received either of the autopsy reports, a twelve-day-old filly died after getting weaker and weaker by continually scouring for six days. Our vet decided to carry out his own autopsy on her, discovering that her stomach lining was perforated with many tiny holes and contained rough spiky matter, including coarse grasses, that should not be in so young a foal. Awaiting the reports from Dublin, we tried to think of any changes we had made in our routine since the last foaling season which might have been the source of this trouble, and also to note the slightest uncommon behaviour in either mares or foals. We noticed that most of the foals which were ill became, at one time or other, slightly lame, as already mentioned, and that one bereaved mare was lame in both forelegs. The mares' droppings were very loose and had an exceptionally strong and unpleasant odour which was especially noticeable when they came back into the stables after grazing in the paddocks. All the foals were scouring for quite a few days before they either died or recovered, the majority for about six days, and those whose dams came in season were even more wretched.

That month of June was like an unending nightmare. We were completely exhausted from nursing sick foals and simultaneously watching new ones arriving and wondering how long they would survive before being stricken with this strange malady. It was the dreadful suspense of not knowing what was causing their illness that made us at one time despair of saving any of the foals. This affair had occurred at a particularly trying time as, since the beginning of March, we had been looking after a young mare who had aborted her foal and had a prolapse of the vagina. It had been replaced and stitched several times, but eventually appeared to be worsening with no hope of ever remaining in place, and as she was in obvious discomfort, it was decided, after a discussion with our vet on 1 June, that he put her to sleep. We had become so attached to her, and it was also the first time we had been faced with such a decision for any of our donkeys, that we were naturally very upset and not at our best to face this latest traumatic experience.

When the reports of the two post-mortem examinations arrived they showed that both animals had ulcerated stomachs which, the laboratory experts suggested, were caused by the presence of fibrous material. We looked anew at our fields and, without doubt, strong fibrous material existed in the pastures, due to the rapid growth of some grass to a stalky stage, and there was also a rich crop of clover. Suddenly many things began to fall into place in our minds. We remembered the plentiful dressing of the quick-action artificial fertiliser which we had spread some weeks before, and the possibility that we had spread other artificial manures in the autumn; our lack of memory on this sounds very inefficient, and it is! Also, although we had given extra supplementary feeding to the first group of foaling mares, we had failed to do so to this second group as we thought that long before they foaled the grass would be plentiful and would thus be sufficient for them.

In our estimation these factors alone would account for the second lot of mares not being in good enough condition to provide adequate milk, so the hungry foals nibbled continually at the tall, spiky, rough grasses, conveniently high enough to tempt them, and which eventually perforated their very young stomachs. The mares tucked into this recent, quick-growing clovery pasture which made what little milk they had over-rich and, as previously stated, their droppings so loose and unpleasantly odorous. With this much understanding garnered we now had some quick thinking to do, resulting in quick action in an effort to save the remaining sick foals and prevent those still to be born from becoming ill.

All during this dreadful period – and truly it was a terrible time, watching day after day, week after week, those dear little creatures 'withering away' as someone described it – our neighbours were wonderful to us. To lose one foal, knowing the cause of death, is distressing enough, but to lose five, one after the other, having nursed them day and night, just watching them become gradually weaker without knowing the whys and wherefores, is a near tragedy. Yet so much assistance of different kinds was offered by so many. A kindly farmer came with his tractor late at night, after working all day cutting his hay, and topped some of our paddocks in the headlights of his tractor until after one in the morning.

Once I returned to the stable to find a young fellow who was helping us at the time 'tying the knot' over a sick foal. This is an old Irish custom whereby a fairly complicated knot is attempted from the centre of a piece of thin cord, leaving the two ends loose once the knot is entwined. The two loose ends are then pulled; should the cord form the attempted knot, it is believed that the animal will recover, but if the cord pulls into a straight length, as it did in this instance, the animal will not recover. Nor did it.

Similar old customs are still remembered and used despite our modern advances. As recently as September last, I received a letter from an Irishwoman in South Africa asking me if the old eighteenth-century cure for cataract of the eyes, drops of asses' bile mixed with water, is still in use. I personally have not come across such a practice but it may well still be in use. However, it was not an ancient remedy but a modern medicine that proved to be of most assistance to us at this time. While chatting one day, our local doctor told us of Ventromil, an excellent aid to humans suffering from ulcers. So, with the concurrence of our open-minded vet, we obtained this product for our small animal medicine chest where it will be stocked for as long as it remains on the market and we breed donkey foals. Its helpful effect was to place a protective layer of a white sticky substance over the sore places in the lining of the stomach, thereby preventing further irritation, while allowing the healing to continue underneath. As we found it to have a slightly constipating effect on the foals we used it in conjunction with liquid paraffin.

All at once the future looked hopeful and so it proved to be. The foals who had only recently started the discomfort dance responded to the new régime and steadily regained their health, though unfortunately one was already too far gone to recover. The last group of mares due to foal were put in a neighbour's nearby fields which had not been dressed with artificial manures. Also the mares had by now benefited from the early summer grazing and had plenty of milk, so our third crop of foals were, like our first lot, free of ailments.

Despite late good fortune, mention of 1969 will always remind us of the sorrows with our foals, as well as the lessons we learned in local husbandry. Never again will we use quick-action artificial fertilisers in fields where young stock are to be kept. We have since used cow manure mixed, in recent years, with a good dressing of seaweed straight up from the shore. We also add Atlantic Kelp to the feed at times: this organic trace element supplement is prepared from pure seaweeds by a nearby factory which, for over thirty years, has processed seaweed gathered over 3,000 miles of the Atlantic coast.

In 1970 we had twenty-six foals and it was wonderful, after the disaster of the previous year, to have had no worries at all with them. The twenty bred foals in 1971 were the most exciting colours we had ever produced, including a completely black filly, Pegeen. Our troubles, I am glad to say, have been few and far between since then.

In order to help other donkey owners, I am here printing in full a paper kindly composed for me by Dr L. B. O'Moore of the Agricultural Institute, Dublin, on suitable ways of coping with feeding these animals:

> In this country donkeys are fed chiefly on grass, either in the form of grazing herbage or conserved as hay. Small amounts of oats and bran are provided for growing and working adult animals. Some owners include other feeding-

ON THE MENU

stuffs, eg crushed barley, beet pulp, molasses, with slight additions of protein concentrates such as linseed meal or soya bean meal.

Grazing may be either on free range or in paddocks. Under free range conditions, an animal can move around over a large area and select those grass species it prefers. In paddock grazing, its choice is limited to what is provided by the sward. Grass for donkeys, and indeed for all equidae, should come from average quality pasture and not from the type used for high-yielding dairy cows or fattening bullocks. A rich clover sward should be eschewed – grazing such pasture has often resulted in scouring and on occasion in severe digestive disturbance with colic.

All equines, including donkeys, are selective grazers. The tendency is for them to overgraze areas of a paddock until these are almost bare, and to ignore other areas which become overgrown and coarse. As horses and donkeys are inclined to pass their droppings and urine on the undergrazed areas, profuse growths of poorer grass species result. Unless pasture management is good, a paddock deteriorates into clumps of coarse inedible grasses, interspersed with closely-cropped bare patches. Good management entails mixed grazing with young cattle – not with sheep which graze too closely – or running the mowing machine over the sward as often as it is necessary. In this case, the long clippings may be left on the pasture. This refers to long clippings only – lawn mown clippings are potentially dangerous, as cases of choking in animals from overgrazing of finely cut grasses occur from time to time.

Hay for donkeys is conserved from permanent pastures which have been shut off for meadowing. It is composed of the leaves and stems of the grasses, clovers and weeds growing on the meadow, and is therefore a reflection of quality of the pasture grazing. Hay must have been well saved and not weathered, musty or mouldy. It should be composed largely of good species – eg perennial ryegrasses, the meadow grasses, timothy and meadow fescue, with some of the allegedly less nutritious strains, eg crested dogstail and sweet vernal. Useful weeds, eg narrow leaf plantain, are desirable. There should be a minimum of poorer species such as bent grass or Yorkshire fog, and obviously no thistle, dock or ragwort (this latter being highly poisonous when included in hay).

Many adult donkeys are kept on grass and reasonably good hay for most of the year. Young animals and those working, eg pulling a light cart or trap, require some hand-feeding as well.

A small quantity of oats mixed with some dry bran in the ratio oats 8 : bran 1, is a satisfactory supplement. Oats are usually fed crushed or rolled. Assuming that an owner has not the facilities for crushing, crushed oats should be purchased in the quantity required from a reliable corn merchant at weekly intervals. These should not be fed after a week or ten days, as after crushing a progressive deterioration sets in – this is slow at first, but in about three weeks rancidity may be obvious.

4 Twinnies

We have had many moments of surprise and happiness on our donkey farm, but none to surpass those we enjoyed in July 1971 when we were unexpectedly blessed with a delightful 'double act'. A short time previously we had sold four donkeys to an open zoo in Northern Ireland and my assistant, John Deakin, had already delivered two of them, a pair of fillies. This zoo, opened for less than a year, impressed John so favourably that he suggested that I should visit it too. So, when the time came to deliver the other two donkeys, a stallion and a gelding, I decided to drive them up myself.

I am seldom away from home in the foaling season but we were then nearing the end of it and there seemed little to keep me at the stud. Breaffy, a brown mare and a much-experienced mother, having produced at least four foals in past years, was due to deliver any day; she knew her job inside out and always accomplished it with great skill, so there was little to worry about there.

John, too, had been with us all season and knew his job thoroughly. Our usual routine at the time of an 'expected event' was simply to keep a watchful eye, give assistance if required and be prepared to make a dash for a vet in an emergency. I had only a slight twinge of apprehension as to whether John, who sleeps the sound sleep of the just, well-known to us from previous efforts to rouse him for his stint of nocturnal duty, would rise to this occasion!

I did not want to delay my journey as the zoo was anxious to have the donkeys, and I hoped to have made the return trip before the start of the Orange Day celebrations in the North only a few days ahead on 12 July. The journey alone with the two asses in the trailer was responsibility enough, without having to negotiate in and out of crowds. Should the donkeys have chanced to hear the sound of a band playing we could have been disgraced forever, as there is little doubt that they would have added their resounding accompaniment. As to whether or not it would have been a welcome contribution to the festivities, I had no wish to find out. So it was decided that I should leave home with my piebald stallion Dubh'sbán (Black and White) on the morning of the eighth, spend the first night with the O'Reilly family, parents of our first donkey girls, collect the gelding Cloud, and stay the second night at my destination in Portrush on the northern coast of Ireland about 270 miles away. A third overnight stop would be needed somewhere on the way back, enabling me to arrive home on 11 July.

The mare Breaffy was, against our normal practice, about a mile from the stud, in a neighbour's field, because grazing-space near home was scarce. During that season we had many foals born from first-foaling mares and, as Breaffy was thought to be less in need of observation than these and the weather fine, we decided to leave her where she was. Breaffy, named incidentally after our local town-land (district), was enormous, but then she always was. Every time she was in foal, though looking only slightly larger than normal, the sages predicted twins. As usual I wagged my head dissentingly and disappointedly at such wishful thinking. While John was loading the stallion two cousins who had stayed the previous night drove me down to have a last peep at the mare. Standing in a field near the edge of

Plate 5 The stud's donkey girls with two of their charges *(Sean Cooke, A.M.P.A.)*

Plate 6 Together as usual, the twins Ome – the black colt on the right – and Omi, a broken-coloured filly

Plate 7 A most unusual painting, W. J. Fennell's 'The Irish Tournament' *(Courtesy of the National Gallery of Ireland)*

Plate 8 This picture depicts the old Irish custom of passing a sick child under and over a donkey a given number of times as a remedy for whooping cough *(Courtesy of The Wellcome Foundation Ltd)*

a cliff, she looked an awesome silhouette, all four legs planted firmly in the sod, balancing, most reluctantly it seemed, her enormous furry paunch. She was not grazing, only giving an odd switch of her tail from time to time as she gazed out to sea, obviously deep in thought and not encouraging any interruption. No doubt she had much to think about, so I left her and journeyed northwards, leaving John to keep his eyes open – or at least one of them!

Early next morning, after a good journey and a comfortable night's rest, I was called unexpectedly to the telephone to hear the rather faint voice of John at the other end of the line. My loud exclamations of, 'It's impossible. I don't believe it, it's not fair to pull my leg at this hour of the morning', were eventually followed, in a different tone of voice by, 'Oh, isn't it quite wonderful, I can't wait to get home', and a thousand instructions of what to do and what not to do, all of which John knew about anyway. My astonished hosts gradually realised that we had had twin foals and that I had not gone completely crazy after all, but I could still hardly believe the news that one was a black/brown colt, the same colour as his dam Breaffy, and the other a broken-coloured filly like the sire Dubh'sbán, the very stallion I was about to deliver that day to Benvarden Zoo, County Antrim.

Seldom have I set out on a journey, as I did that morning, with more of a wish to get it over and return home. Yet, interlaced with the excitement of the births, was a slight feeling of sadness always present when any of our large family are about to leave us. Even when we are as sure as we can ever be that our donkeys are going to a good home, as was the case then, there is nonetheless a sense of loss at the parting. After all, each animal has been, to a greater or lesser degree, a part of our life, and they take a part of it with them.

Arriving at the zoo, we three were welcomed most courteously by everyone there, and while the stallion and his companion were being installed in their new quarters, I was taken to see Caro and Miss Bonny, the two fillies we had sent up previously. They too bestowed on me a warm welcome, conveyed by those wonderful puffy-snuffly noises all donkey owners know, or should know. It was good to see them so well and contented. They were in a large enclosure with a few other donkeys, not far from their cousins the zebras, and were receiving graciously the attentions showered on them by the public as though they were the only animals there. The zoo was all I had been led to believe, the animals being beautifully cared for and seemingly more contended than in most other zoos. Here were people who knew their animals and cared for them with affection; I need have little fear leaving our donkeys in this environment.

With thoughts of the twins pushed forcibly into the background by so much else of interest, I spent a most interesting evening with the zoo proprietors, discussing the animals and learning many fascinating events about life among them. However, I had every intention of getting home the next day, sidestepping the extra night away, in order to view the two new arrivals as soon as possible, and so I rose early as I intended to break my return journey to search out a fine, broken-coloured stallion, Pepito, and a grey/brown mare which had been sold a year or so previously to a co-operative concern. As I had never succeeded in getting a response to my correspondence as to how these two fared I did not let anyone know of my intended visit.

I found the location without difficulty but was disappointed to hear that the mare was too far away for me to see that day. I did, however, see the stallion, who was alone in a large, isolated field, looking sad and neglected. Upset by his condition I gave some advice for his future welfare but, while the employee who accompanied me was sympathetic, he doubted that these suggestions would be favourably received by those in control. I explained that stallions seldom thrive if left alone, especially in the spring and summer months when they should be serving mares, and are restless anyway. The company of a gelding is ideal as the two can romp around together, giving the stallion companionship and enabling him to get rid of excess energy if he is not mated often. It was a disturbing visit, even though I was most cordially received. Intending to pursue the matter further by letter and telephone, I left on my homeward journey, flying along country roads with my empty trailer and trying, like the crows, to make the straightest and shortest trail to Breaffy and her 'twinnies', but alas, after bumping along for hours on my uncharted course, I arrived home in the dark, too late to make their acquaintance.

The sun was up waiting for me the next morning and, in waiting, he had not been idle. Glowing with warmth this early July morning he had ousted the lazy dew and dispersed it in the mellow summer air, sent his beams dancing over the sea, skipping and a-glittering on the sparkling waters, while his rays, still soft in the youthful day, spread benignly over all, helping mother nature arrange a perfect setting on which to show off her latest works of art. We all have some very special days in our lives, days which we remember time and again with particular delight and happiness. The first sight of the twins on that glorious summer morning marked for me one such day. These two strangely-coloured, tiny, fluffy, long-eared miracles of creation, moving in little jerky steps around their still portly looking dam, yet venturing forth impishly to proffer their incredibly smooth, creamy, soft muzzles as a first offer of friendship, were to me then the eighth wonder of the world.

Perhaps I have gone into the clouds, so I had better come down to earth and recall what I then learned of the twins' birth. According to John's wife, he sprang out of bed at the astonishingly early hour of 6am. Thinking that the house, at least, must be afire, she anxiously bestirred herself, only to be reassured that no such apparent drama was afoot. John is still not sure why he rose so early as he had seen Breaffy late the previous night when she was still alone, deep in thought and deep in shape. Dressing hastily, he jumped into his car and, rounding a turn of the road near where a bridge crosses the inlet of sea opposite the field, he saw Breaffy standing up with a tiny, white object near her on the grass. With a fervent prayer that all was well with this, his first solo care of a donkey's accouchment, he parked the car out of sight and quietly made his way to her. To his delight, he found a beautifully marked black/brown-and-white filly foal, just out of its membrane bag, still wet, but very much alive and alert. Vastly relieved he waited for the little one to begin the literally staggering performance of legs shooting out in all directions and terrifying falls which always precedes their first 'stand-up' in life and, at the same time, removes from the hooves the rubber-like substance which nature provides to cushion their hardness before and during birth.

Occupied in this direction, John did not immediately become aware of Breaffy's further activities, but when he did he received quite a jolt to his nervous system – she was lying down again and quite obviously in labour! The likes of this John most certainly had not seen before; to go for help now or to stay was the vital question. He told himself he would stay – spoken like a man, John – and soon was rewarded by the appearance of two little black hooves, one slightly in front of the other, enclosed in a bubble-like bag emerging from the mare. After a short rest, Breaffy's labour started again and she brought forth the head, nose first, resting along the upper parts of the fore legs. Yet another good rest before her final strenuous effort produced the body, followed by the hind legs which slipped out easily, all encased in a bag of membrane which, broken in the process of foaling, showed a tiny black colt foal taking his first breaths of the bracing seaside air. So it was twins – O-me, O-mi!

The mare, relieved of her heavy burden, sat up and gazed in astonishment from one to the other of her twin foals. Rising laboriously to her feet, she inspected them both, licking them approvingly for a while until, painfully reminded of her next task, she wandered off to evacuate the placenta or afterbirth, which made her more comfortable. Now came the time when novice donkey 'midwives' could easily lose their heads as once the second, black colt had accomplished the acrobatic feats which would eventually get him up squarely, if not firmly, on all four legs, a most important part of the proceedings had to be carefully carried out. John deftly gathered the offspring together for that most important ceremony, their first meal from Mum. Careful supervision is most necessary at this stage to see that each foal receives its fair quota of the mare's first milk after parturition, the colostrum. He cleverly manoeuvred them so that each little one got a teat apiece and thereby their fair share of the precious liquid, normally rich in vitamins A and D. Deprived of this first milk, foals could face many future difficulties as it acts as a natural purgative, clearing away the accumulated faecal matter known as meconium and also supplying antibodies which protect the young animal against various bacteria and viruses.

This vital action happily organised, John then had to carry out the somewhat distasteful job of clearing up the afterbirths, as donkeys do not attempt to devour them as do many other animals. Then he weighed the foals for our records, a complicated process of addition and subtraction carried out on bathroom scales, by noting first of all the person's weight, then with the foal held in his arms their combined weight, then taking away the person you just thought of to get the foal's weight: a mighty Pythagorean deduction, you will agree! Anyway, it summed up the filly foal to have been 42lb and the colt 37lb at birth.

Fearing that Breaffy might not leave her precious babies to go to the drinking trough, John brought some water to her and then, having coped most competently with an unexpected and unusual situation, he turned for home to spread the good news and to have a well-earned breakfast.

Breaffy was an excellent mother and looked after her babies with great care. Having brought them home to our front paddock, we were able to participate closely in these early months of their lives and observe their day-to-day habits. The news of the twin births soon spread locally and many people came to pay their respects. When these respects were paid in kind, though not encouraged by us, they were greedily received by Breaffy whose large tum seemed like a bottomless pit. Although she never seemed to stop eating her two rapacious youngsters took all the milk she could give, so that she can seldom have felt replete. A most maternal mare who, although after the loss of her second foal when only three weeks old had cried moanfully and tearfully for days, was surprisingly not overly possessive of the twins. She seemed to know that something special had happened and was inordinately proud of them, only getting anxious if something startled her, when she would then purposefully install herself between them and whatever it was that had caused her concern. Perhaps a strange barking dog or a noisy child would upset her and, once on the defensive, nothing could circumvent the formidable fortification that was mother Breaffy.

All friendly attentions were graciously received by the trio who lapped up the copious cuddling and fondling from us all. These were halcyon days, the weather was glorious and, with twinnies on our doorstep there was never a dull moment. Foals playing together at anytime are enchanting, but these two had a ball. Ome, the little black colt, was the instigator of all mischief and a right little bully too. Though younger and smaller than his sister Omi, he would torment her until she had to run for it, then off the two would go tearing around the paddock, their tiny hooves flaying the ground as they careered along at an alarming speed. Such was their headlong progress that sometimes even Beaffy would become worried and waddle over to reprimand her offspring. On the few occasions when the naughty little black lad was getting the worst of the sport, Mum would always take his side. Being the same colour she probably felt closer to him, or perhaps he just went and 'told tales' on his sister, like some small boys do! Whatever the reason, that upstart little fellow got his own way more often than not. As soon as order was restored, the two subsided exhausted and, after a refreshing sup, flopped down together – always together – to sleep it off.

Then, when the twins were nearly five weeks old, Omi became unwell. A feeling of near-panic enveloped us all, for this little family had weaved itself so thoroughly into our way of life that even the flicker of a thought that anything could happen to them made us aghast. All our stock were precious to us, but that little pair, first by their rarity and later by their sheer delightfulness, had claimed more than their fair share of our attention. Omi's look of apathy was the first indication that anything was wrong. All too soon we noticed the familiar 'discomfort dance', though we were grateful to see that she only moved from one foot to the other infrequently and did not draw her legs up under her in that clench-like way which indicated greater pain. She was also scouring and had a slight temperature. We called the vet who treated her against the effects of a possible chill and other likely ailments.

A very worrying ten days followed with the foal under constant supervision. We dosed her to clear up the scours and then gave her liquid paraffin to guard against constipation. Once again daily doses of Ventromil were called for. She was allowed no roughage at all and one or other of us stayed beside her all day in the fields to see that she did not swallow anything that might act as an internal irritant. At night the trio were confined to a stable, with Breaffy's hay hung in a bag in one corner, guarded by planks so that the foals could not get at the wisps of hay falling to the ground. Without a doubt we were blessed by the perfect weather and by our ever-kindly friends and neighbours. Someone let us use his nearby field, thereby making our routine much easier. All gave us their moral support and, in a couple of weeks, Omi was restored to health. Many times since we have been asked 'what ailed her'. We could not pin-point the trouble, but it was certainly of a digestive nature.

When Ome was twelve weeks old we had him gelded to enable us to keep the twins together always. At the time of writing they are over three years old and have had no other health problems. We did not wean them until they were nearly two years old, and then only eleven days before Breaffy presented them with a fine dark-brown sister, weighing over 56lb, called Doonagore.

The twins' birthday, falling as it does in the middle of our tourist season, calls for celebrations. For their first one we made a birthday cake with candles and all the visitors of the day came to see them, somehow or other managing to produce tit-bits which were offered with birthday greetings! The children were delighted with all the fuss and excitement – and so were the twinnies! Their third birthday was a watery affair as it poured with rain for days before and after, so all festivities were abandoned. For their fourth birthday we hope to have them trained and ready to take some of their visitors on an outing in double-harness.

Donkey twins are comparatively rare but it is difficult to obtain details of their incidence. As with humans, twins tend to run in families, but correct detailed records on the breeding of donkeys have not been in existence long enough for us to give information on the percentage of twins born to them. In horse mares about 3 per cent conceive twin foetuses but these are mostly aborted, only ·01 per cent of them producing healthy twins.

Identical twins are the result of a fertilised egg which has divided in two. Ordinary twins follow the fertilisation of two eggs. In cattle the two eggs can come from the same ovary, develop in one horn of the womb and even share the same blood circulation. If the twins born are of the same sex all is well, but should they be of different sexes the female's reproductive system will be upset by the male's sex hormones and she will become what is called a 'sterile freemartin'. I have been unable to establish whether this applies to donkeys or not, but I find the following statement from an article on 'Freemartinism' by Messrs B. L. Gledhill and B. Gustaffson in the *International Encyclopedia of Veterinary Medicine* (W. Green & Son, Edinburgh, 1966) most interesting: 'There are many reports which strongly suggest that freemartinism occurs most frequently and is most severe in the bovine species but, in fact, it does occur in other species, notably porcine, ovine, caprine and equine.' They also state 'the origin of the term "freemartin" is unknown but the condition which it describes has been recognised since biblical times'.

I have heard of five other sets of donkey twins in recent years but only have details of two pairs. One pair were broken-coloured fillies, both of which have since bred healthy foals. The others were of different sexes and different shades of the same colour, but too young yet to breed. Of our twins, I have not yet tried to breed from Omi, though she first came into season when barely a year old, and has continued to do so periodically ever since.

5 Open to the Public

Looking back over more than a decade of life with our donkeys, it is difficult to remember events in their correct sequence, though certain incidents, such as the birth of the twins, stand out like beacons. Public interest in the stud, first aroused by the arrival of our foals, has grown over the years since then, though we did not think, however remotely, to capitalise on it in those early days.

In the mid-sixties we were busy taking in visiting mares from all over the country to be serviced by our stallions which, at that time, were the only donkey stallions advertised as being at stud in this part of the world. Our great interest in breeding donkeys of different and mixed colours was a big draw so that owners of the more numerous grey, brown and black mares brought them to our broken-coloured and white stallions in the hope of getting a broken-coloured (skewbald and piebald) foal, or even a chestnut one, though that colour was not as popular then as it is now. When the news leaked out that we had paid a three-figure price for a young colt from County Limerick, from which we hoped to breed broken-coloured stock later on, a newspaper reporter paid us a visit to write an article on our activities. This, of course, helped widen the interest in donkeys. Although we were not the first to own broken-coloured stock in Ireland, I would hazard a guess that we were the first to breed them selectively. Donkey lovers in England had been willing purchasers of the few broken-coloureds that had turned up now and then, as they were of the multitudes of plain-coloured donkeys which were regularly exported there. It was perhaps the realisation that donkeys could have such a surprisingly varied livery that first helped to draw general attention to them, other than as working animals, and we soon established a thriving trade in providing donkeys for good homes at home and abroad.

During the spring and early summer of 1967 we had a most attractive crop of foals which came in many sizes, shapes and colours, keeping both us and the growing numbers of visitors totally absorbed. It was wonderful to see such an interest in the donkeys, who revelled in the attentions received. Then, one day in late summer there was tremendous excitement and some nervous trepidation when it was learned that a television crew wished to film at the stud. As most people know, photographing animals is very painstaking work and donkeys, with their habitual curiosity, insist on trying to discover what is inside the camera. We thought it best to put many of the mares and foals in the front paddock and let the enterprising cameramen wander around among them so that both parties could get used to each other. The plan worked well, resulting in some excellent photography of the donkeys eating, sleeping, playing, getting up, lying down, rolling and making friends with the team.

I was a bit nonplussed though to hear that the crew wished to record a donkey braying. As mares seldom bray, and then mostly for a specific reason as when they are 'in season', or when distressed at periods such as weaning time, it looked as if we should have to bring a stallion on the scene, as they will trumpet away at the drop of a hat. The louder the bray, the better it would suit the recording machine, we were told, so a stalwart member of staff went off to fetch Pepito, the broken-coloured stallion mentioned in the previous chapter, who had quite a reputation for enthusiastic musical talent. The plan was to walk him up the drive in sight of the mares and alongside the van containing the TV recorder. Never a lad to be backward in coming forward where the ladies were concerned was our Pepito so, to be on the safe side, two men were posted in the drive near the railings to help impede his expected charge ahead, while we all stood well back so as not to be deafened and to enable the recorder to take the full blast of his bray.

Through the gate came Pepito, as calm as you please and, much to our chagrin, walked quietly past mares and recorder van into the yard without a toot, obviously on his best behaviour for the visitors. Very perplexed after such a let-down we could only turn him round and walk him back again. Ah, now he could have an uninterrupted look at the occupants of the paddock from the moment he stepped out of the yard and, though straining at the leash, he puffed and panted until he had filled his lungs to capacity then let out the mother and father of a hee-haw right alongside the recorder van. Such a bray, if replayed in full audibility would have shattered the walls of any studio, but what care he, was he not a fine tuneful fellow and had he not given of his best?

The television team, headed by Cathal O'Shannon, seemed more than satisfied with this particular donkey serenade and we were all very happy with the results of that day's work in a fifteen-minute showing on Frank Hall's Radio Telefís Éireann programme. The popularity of that first programme, still remembered by many visitors, did much to stimulate future important decisions we had to make about our life here, and the interest it aroused helped us enormously. During the following years, we have had three continental and two English television crews here, all helping to publicise the stud overseas. It has been amusing to note that when the team arrive, all work is first discussed and looked at in a most business-like way, with an apparent urgency to get this job over and on to the next. Yet in no time at all after their introduction to the donkeys, reporters and cameramen alike are relaxed, highly intrigued with their subject and spend ages just wandering around inspecting our donkey trappings so that when the time comes to say goodbye the parting between them, the donkeys, and us is always a reluctant one.

Most of 1968 was spent in writing my first book, *The Irish Donkey*, which included details of our early experiences in breeding donkeys, some personal observations on their behaviour and a little history on their ancestors. To help me out during this busy time we employed our first young female assistant who was straightway labelled a 'donkey girl', a title which has been automatically attached to all our teenage lady helpers ever since. Throughout this period the general public and many friends continued to call and see us, much to our pleasure. All too often however, just as we wished to entertain friends, we would have to rush off to make refreshments for strangers who had travelled long distances to see the stud – and to come here in the days before the car-ferry across the Shannon joined us to the main coastal road was a tiring journey from most places. We decided therefore that next season we would make some alterations and an addition to our small summer-house so that we could sell refreshments and donkey souvenirs from there. Now we would be officially open to the public.

At a friend's suggestion we approached Bord Fáilte, our Tourist Board, who were most encouraging and helped us to get started. By early 1970 the summer-house alterations were complete with the nucleus of the donkey shop and adjacent refreshment counter already there, plus two outside cloakrooms and an office in the making. Not having previously considered how to advertise the venture and where to find suitable merchandise, we were at first a little daunted by the prospect. Nevertheless, minerals and ice-creams were not difficult to obtain, and copies of my book were put boldly on display alongside a few dozen single records of 'Delaney's Donkey' sung by Val Doonican. We had made a start.

News of our activities was getting around as we were soon to discover when, unexpectedly one day, there came a telephone call from helpful allies to know whether we could take a bus-load of twenty-five people for coffee the following morning. The answer was decidedly in the affirmative. It had been no trouble at all to confirm such a party on the telephone but once the receiver was down pandemonium broke out. How could we manage twenty-five people together? We were not geared to serve morning coffee – did we have enough cups? Perhaps they did not like music or reading and, if so, what could they possibly buy in the shop? The prospect looked far from rosy, until we remembered that our *spécialité* was, after all, the donkey, and that the paddock held the first foals of the season. Heartened by this thought we leaped into action, rearranged our own dining-room to accommodate the overflow of guests should the weather prove unkind, unearthed every cup in the place and purchased large tins of instant coffee. A plea for help to some ceramic artists with whom we were already negotiating, brought forth, almost miraculously, ashtrays with the stud name engraved on them and a few other odds and ends to adorn the almost empty shelves of the shop.

Next day with sighs of relief at the fine, though windy weather we excitedly awaited our first bus-load of visitors who turned out to be French travel agents. They were charming guests, most understanding about our beginners' efforts at a commercial enterprise, and completely captivated by the foals which, excited by the wind and their appreciative audience, gave a fine display of high jinks.

Encouraged by the evident enjoyment of visitors so experienced in the tourist trade, our hopes rose for the future. This unscheduled visit had shown us that we must make hasty arrangements to accommodate visitors in greater numbers than hitherto considered, not an easy thing to do at this stage as we did not wish to have the added expense of building a tearoom until we discovered if the venture as previously planned turned out to be a success. Yet, if we were to attract bus-loads of visitors, we could not leave those who were unable to squeeze into the tiny shop crouching under their umbrellas in stormy weather, or discontentedly sheltering in a bus while their fellow passengers devoured the grub. After much thought we

OPEN TO THE PUBLIC

decided to take out that side of the bay window in our dining-room which was opposite the shop only about 20ft from it, and replace it with a door. With little more to do than remove what we needed for our personal use, we then covered the table and sideboards with attractive plastic cloths and the room was available to the public. As the weather was excellent for most of that first season our guests were able to sit in the garden on the old three-legged milking stools which were also used as mini-tables, so the extra accommodation was hardly ever called upon. While the visitors took tea or coffee and the home-made cakes now added to our scanty menu, served on a handy TV tray, they could watch the donkeys giving rides to children and taking them out in the trap, or they simply sat in the sun watching the mares and foals which, as usual, provided great entertainment.

Finally, a brochure was hastily produced and our inauguration into public life was soon down in black and white for all to see. The important decision as to who would perform the official opening ceremony was not a difficult one to make, for Spanish Point had a celebrity of its own, none other than our government's Minister for External Affairs, Dr Patrick Hillery, who lived within an ass's roar of us. Although he was particularly busy at this time he kindly agreed and suggested 8 August as a suitable day.

The next most involved decision was, of course, who to invite to the opening ceremony as ideally we would like to have asked the whole countryside and more. Eventually we resolved to ask our few immediate neighbours and anyone locally who had assisted us with our project. Both the Protestant vicar and the Roman Catholic priest of the parish were invited to come and bless the venture. Also welcomed were about a dozen blind people from the area, for whom we now have an annual party.

Looking after the donkeys themselves is a full-time job in the summer as it is the time when our scheduled foals are born. Both dam and foal require attention, even if only to give them the personal visit every day which we consider essential. It is obvious that the earlier you can treat an illness, the easier it is to cure, and this is particularly important with donkey foals because while in health they are very gay, in sickness they get dispirited and go downhill very quickly. We also fitted in visits from interested parties so there was plenty to occupy us as the days flew by until Saturday, 8 August dawned dry and warm.

Soon the afternoon was with us and saw a table and chairs outside the front door on the wide semi-circular part of our driveway, between house and paddock, overlooked by the shop, awaiting the arrival of those who were to partake in the ceremony. There was also room for our favourite trap-donkey, Alana, to stand harnessed near the railings. Another donkey, who shall be nameless for reasons to be disclosed later, was dressed in a bridle and carried on his back a pair of turf-baskets which were full of children's toys wrapped in gaily-coloured paper to hide their identity, called 'Surprise Packets'. The paddock boasted a fair share of the mares and foals and the tea was laid out inside the house. All seemed in order, the only discordant note – or notes – coming from the stallions some fields away who, we are sorry to say, were not invited as their manners are not always up to party standard, especially with lady donkeys present in the paddock.

When all were assembled, Dr Hillery, who had driven from Dublin nearly 200 miles away just to be with us, spoke most encouragingly of our unique organisation, expressing the hope that it would attract many tourists and lead to more interest in and care of all donkeys, animals so often associated with Ireland yet at that time rather thin on the ground in our country. Declaring the stud officially open he sat down to loud applause which was greatly appreciated by us, but not unfortunately by the unnamed carrier of the panniers who, startled by the ovation, threw not only his heels in the air but also most of the surprise packets. Not a very good prelude to the ecumenical blessing of which we were so badly in need and which was now about to be respectfully requested. As the hilarity died down, quelled by the agonised looks from some of us, the ceremonies continued and both the vicar and the parish priest prayed for God's blessings on us all.

With the stud now officially open, what better way to celebrate the occasion than to give our distinguished guest a drive in the donkey-trap. Alana, a most placid animal, was nevertheless conscious of all the excitement around her and to guard against possible loss of our enterprising Foreign Minister, certainly the first Foreign Minister to open a donkey stud, one of our donkey-girls acted as escort, while the cameras clicked away recording our jovial caper for posterity, as well as many other happenings on this our Opening Day.

That first open season proved a never ending source of entertainment to us. No one really knew what to expect from the visitors and I doubt if, in those early days, they knew what to expect from us, in spite of the information we had placed here and there explaining what we had to offer, where tickets were required and their individual cost, our opening and closing times and any other relevant facts. About halfway along the short drive which runs from the main road up to the front of our house and shop, between the paddock railings and the garden wall, we placed a small caravan from which we could sell entrance tickets. We did sell a few tickets to the more venturesome visitors who were willing to risk a 5p entrance charge if anyone of us happened to be in the caravan when they arrived, but we soon realised that both caravan and entrance tickets were formidable barriers to the public, especially those who came in a family party, so the caravan was removed to the yard and the entrance fee banished forever. Should a family of four come to the stud, one child may want a donkey ride whilst the other may go on a general conducted tour. Individual tickets are purchased for both these events. Meanwhile the parents may just wish to sit quietly in the car on the driveway and we could hardly feel justified in charging for this. The decision gave us many a frustrating moment in those early days, as well as a laugh or two.

We did not have enough visitors at first to warrant keeping someone continually in the shop, so when we either heard or saw a car coming up the drive the next person on duty was called for

Plate 9 Dr Patrick Hillery, Irish Minister for External Affairs, seen here with the author and donkey Alana at the official opening to the public of the Spanish Point stud in August 1970 *(Clare Champion)*

Plate 10 The late Mr Erskine Childers, then President of the Irish Republic, and his wife with the author and her husband (partially blocked). Mrs Childers is here fondling the foal Rita, born on the morning of their visit, which now bears her name *(Wilson, Ennis)*

Plate 11 All I want is a bit of peace and quiet ... the cat, Mister Ister, in an un'ass'ailable position! *(Gail McKechnie)*

Plate 12 The Lord Swinfen with foal Paprika in a rainbow donkey rug, the forerunner of the popular rainbow sweaters on sale in the donkey shop. Note the Horrible Dog taking his ease in the background

and had to leave whatever he was doing to attend to the visitors. It was simply maddening to find that many people just drove up, turned round and went off again without getting out. Many times since we would have been half glad to see this happen, when there has been a large crowd to attend to and an overworked staff, but in those early days the excitement of any arrival was intense and the sale of anything in the shop, even for a few pence, was a triumph. We tried to think of ways of preventing these curiosity visits and I remembered an idea of friends who, when their driveway near a lonely beach was used in a similar fashion, put up a sign reading 'Beware of the Agapanthus'. On consideration I felt that this could have a two-way effect, so decided that inaction was best.

One amusing incident from those early days occurred when we were leaning on the paddock rails talking to neighbours and a car with a young couple in it drove up. Our friends, as excited as we were murmured 'business', but unfortunately they spoke too soon as the inmates of the car gave a quick look, then turned around and drove off. Feeling a bit deflated, after a derisive chuckle we went inside for a sherry. About twenty minutes later, seeing the same car coming up the drive, we raised our glasses in triumph, watching appraisingly from the sitting-room window as the occupants got out and walked towards the shop. But the glasses remained clutched in our hands as the 'visitors' veered leftwards to the cloakrooms from where they emerged a few moments later, got back in the car and drove off again. We, after a moment of stunned silence, collapsed with laughter and downed our drinks. Of course, there is absolutely no reason why anyone should not simply use the loos and go straight out again – most of us have behaved in a similar manner at hotels or other places open to the public – and these days we never mind a jot if people just come in and only look around. But in those early days when we were all so earnestly intent on making a go of this first-time venture, we were alert to every potentiality, for there was so much we had to learn.

News of our existence was not widely known in the tourist world as yet and, as we lived a long way from most bus terminals, we did not have many regular coach-loads of visitors except for the regular Thursday bus from Limerick. This leaves there early in the morning once a week from June to the end of August on a round tour of local resorts, calling in on us for afternoon tea en route. Not until between noon and one o'clock on the same day, after a telephone call to the hotel where the tour stops for lunch, can we know how many people to expect each Thursday. The figures could range from seven to seventy, though once, or perhaps twice, we have had to cater for a larger number who arrived in two buses. The smaller numbers relate chiefly to the early part of the year, the high-season average being thirty to forty passengers. The time of arrival varies too, as they take longer over their sightseeing if the weather is good, but they usually arrive between 4.15 and 5.15pm and stay long enough for refreshment, a browse in the shop and a visit to the donkeys.

Once we were asked to take two teas out to the bus which always parks outside the front gate. Thinking the teas were for invalids we hastened out to find two apparently healthy young ladies walking around inside. These girls, who were sisters, thanked us profusely, explaining that they were quite terrified of animals and would never willingly go anywhere where they might come across them face to face – and a donkey stud was no exception!

Sometimes catering for this regular bus can prove hazardous, especially at the peak of the holiday season. The news soon gets around that our home cooking is abundant and not a minute old. As Thursday is a half-day holiday in many nearby towns an avalanche of people can have visited the stud before the bus arrives, so we have to try carefully to balance the day ahead. The weather conditions, always to the forefront of our minds, are scrutinised even more carefully, as is news of any local attractions which would affect the numbers we may expect, for while we do not wish the travellers to go away hungry, neither do we wish to be left with a surfeit of tea-time food which is only tasty when really fresh as learnt one never-to-be-forgotten afternoon. We were expecting the last bus of the season and had been informed that there were forty-five visitors aboard. With everything prepared we waited long past the expected time of arrival, when suddenly a cry rang out that the bus was coming down the road. Sure enough, down the road it came, and down the road it continued, right past our gate and with never a glance from its occupants, steadily onwards clean out of sight. Stupefied we turned from the windows, looked at each other and then at the counter loaded high with tea-time goodies, the same thought in every head – what do we do with all this? Why on earth did they not stop?

The day and the season were almost gone, and so too was our sense of humour. It was too much, we were not going to put up with this kind of treatment, how dare they do such a thing, something must be done about it and at once too. So after I had marched to the telephone armed with some very nasty words which needed an outing, it was thwarting to be given the perfectly rational explanation that the regular driver was ill and that the temporary one must have overlooked us. As we slowly regained our equilibrium, we were delighted to discover that we had not after all lost the toss as hungry visitor after hungry visitor poured in until there was not a morsel left on the counter. Isn't it strange how a sense of humour can suddenly return!

While everything possible is done to cater for our visitors they must, in the natural order of things, take second place to the donkeys. The months in which we are open to the public without appointment coincide with our busiest months at the stud as it is during this time that our official matings take place and the foals of last year's marriages are born. I use the word 'official' advisedly as there are occasional accidents of birth which can only be termed otherwise. We once had three pretty fillies bred by us and a white one which we had bought, all two-year-olds, which we did not wish to mate until the following year and then to chosen stallions. These were thought to be segregated far away and in a place safe from their prospective bridegrooms. And so they were, but not from the local Casanova of whose existence we were unaware. It was a bitter disappointment to us when we learnt what had happened as the unofficial matings curtailed an experimental breeding programme we had in mind for at least three of them. Totally in disgrace the naughty ladies were kept together under special observation as no one knew when to expect these first foals conceived on the wrong side of the fence. It was when some visitors heard mention of 'the field where the unmarried mothers were kept' that the mares became celebrities and were added to the itinerary of our conducted tour. In due course some little so and so's were born, so utterly enchanting that all was forgiven.

Though we go about our donkey duties during visiting hours, often appreciating the interest taken by the public, there are times when it is not so welcome. A completely unexpected interruption one evening gave me the fright of a lifetime. A stranger appeared at the half-door of the stable while I was taking a donkey's temperature. Looking up to answer his query I naturally took my eyes from the thermometer which had been inserted into the appropriate passage. When I looked down again a few seconds later the thermometer had simply vanished. Even as I write this I shudder anew remembering the horrifying possibility of just where that implement might have got to: the overwhelming sense of relief at finding it in the straw bedding scarcely mitigated the impact of the shock received.

While we were caring for the orphan foal mentioned in Chapter 2, a large party of teenage boys came to visit us by arrangement. Though we were all very conscious that we had a little invalid in the stable we did our best to entertain our guests and not let our anxiety affect their reception. Unfortunately, while the boys were here, the foal's condition deteriorated and he needed immediate attention from two people, so we had to leave our guests on their own for the rest of their visit. By this time they knew what was going on and kept peeping into the stable to enquire about the patient until we suggested it was best for him to be left as quiet as possible. Still busy when they departed, we were unable to bid them farewell, and later on we worried lest they had felt neglected and might not have understood that what we were doing could not have been delegated.

It was a great relief when, some days later, we received a charming letter from the lady in charge of the party, saying how much they had enjoyed the outing and enquiring especially after the foal. We greatly appreciated their understanding, and it was good to know that these young people realised our priorities in such a situation.

Dealing with the public day after day during many months of the year can be very exacting, especially when life is busy and we are all working under pressure. There have been occasions, though so few that we can remember them, when we have been tempted to forget that 'a soft answer turneth away wrath'. One day, for example, a family arrived quarrelling and remained arguing noisily for some while before getting out of the car. After a conducted tour, they asked for a refund of their tickets because there were only donkeys on view! What we replied is not recorded.

Another time, about three or four hired car-loads of fella-me-lads blew in and asked to see the 'daankees'. When invited to take tickets for the tour they decided they did not want to bother after all and departed hurriedly, to be seen shortly afterwards clambering over the wall and jostling some of our youngest animals who, taking fright, had bolted in all directions – as did our troublesome guests when they saw us coming!

A few isolated incidents like these are little to complain of, especially when we have a lot of excited children about the place. We do have one strict rule, however, and this is that no one is allowed to visit the donkeys unless accompanied by one of us or special permission has been previously obtained. While all our donkeys are friendly and any unpleasantness is highly unlikely unless deliberately and intensely provoked, accidents can happen anywhere and in any place. So, while we owe the public all possible care, we also owe care to our animals and are determined to guard their good reputation.

6   Fair Winds and Foul Weather

Towards the end of 1973 we heard that the then newly elected President of Ireland, Erskine Childers, planned to pay an official visit to a nearby seaside resort, so we wrote and suggested that if he could manage to fit in a private visit to the donkey stud also, we would feel both honoured and delighted. Back came a reply from his secretary saying that the president would certainly call to see us and asking what plans we had in mind for his reception.

The prospect of this visit gave us something exciting to look forward to during the appalling weather conditions of that autumn and winter, the most wet and windy winter season experienced on our part of the coast in living memory. Farmers all around had the greatest difficulty in caring for their stock and our young assistant, Noel Barker, did a Herculean job looking after our large herd of donkeys. Day after day, battling against blustery winds and drenching rain in an effort to get enough fodder to the animals in their fields while almost up to the waist in mud, is no enviable job. There were times when he had not got a dry pair of trousers left and had to borrow some from my husband. As Noel is the taller of the two by quite a few inches, it added some fun to those cheerless days to see him in his minitrousers. Eventually fisherman's waders proved the answer.

As fodder of any kind became scarce and expensive, there were times when we actually wondered if we could manage to keep the animals alive at all. Many people lost domestic stock from starvation and exposure. There were great losses of hay; we alone lost no less than twenty-seven acres of it and had to buy large quantities which sometimes arrived as late as 11pm then had to be unloaded and distributed by artificial light. Month after month this wretched weather continued, preventing us from carrying out our normal attentions to the donkeys so that their hooves grew into odd shapes and their coats looked unkempt. The in-foal mares received priority attention being brought to the fields nearer home, but this meant that these fields, usually rested in the winter, had little preparation for our summer season.

At last, in March, the weather cleared and there was a frantic rush to get everything ready for opening the stud as usual at Easter, and to prepare for the president's visit some weeks later. A priority was to remove the mounds of manure which had accumulated outside the donkeys' shelters during the bad weather when no vehicle could enter the fields without getting stuck in the mud. Visit after visit from the blacksmith was necessary to get the donkeys' sodden and sometimes twisted hooves back into shape and the grooming required was overwhelming. Cascades of paint flowed like waterfalls over house, shop, stables, shelters, railings, gates and anything that caught the eye of Joe, our painter, whose wife was to cater so efficiently during the summer months ahead. My daughter, Coral, recently returned home after many years in Kenya, took charge of the shop and with the sporadic help of my mother, young Sean during school breaks, and Mrs Doyle and Michael, both with us intermittently for over twelve years, we were able once more to open up to the public in a rather haphazard fashion.

The new foals out front were a particular asset just then, as we were expecting a stream of American visitors who would not have time for a tour. These were employees of a sports goods manufacturing company which, pleased with the year's financial results, had given sixty-eight of the staff, together with their wives, a week's holiday in Ireland with all expenses paid. The organisers had hired a fleet of chauffeur-driven Mercedes and arranged a kind of treasure hunt, which took the holiday-makers round a large area from Shannon Airport seeking answers to questions and procuring odd objects like a feather, plant or special shell. One of the answers they needed was the names of our twin donkeys, Ome, Omi. Most of the Americans stayed on at Spanish Point for tea and there was great hilarity each time a fresh car-load of the party drove up as they all surreptitiously tried to find out who had the answer to this or that query. We too were drawn into the fun as they plied us with questions, the answers to which we were not supposed to disclose.

Another similar affair was a German caravan rally in which the participants had to call at certain places located all over the country and obtain a signed certificate from each place as proof of their call. The first callers had very little knowledge of the English language and we had even less of the German, so it took much searching through our English/German dictionary, and many gesticulations before we agreed to sign our name to the document with even a modicum of confidence without seeming ungracious. Our next caravan-club members some days later did speak English and they were able to confirm our confidence and trace for us an outline of the plan they had to follow.

Other groups from overseas came en masse in coaches, like the German golfers who were touring round playing at all the best Irish courses. These buses were, admittedly, different from the general run of hire-coaches which we usually saw, as these were owned by the leader of the group who had converted part of one into a dining-cum-sitting-room with a millionaire's bar, to which we were invited for drinks served by a smart steward. Another coach brought a party of French farmers and I also recall a coach full of stalwart-looking German policemen who, thinking we were a charitable institution, offered us a generous contribution towards the upkeep of the donkeys! Sadly, we were away from home when a group arrived from Oklahoma, and consequently it was an unexpected pleasure to receive their appreciative letters from across the Atlantic, especially as some of our favourite donkey friends dwell over there.

The seasonal activities continued, though frustrated too often by the fickle climatic conditions which once again enveloped us in no uncertain manner. As the day of the president's visit drew near and our plans for his reception crystallised, the only danger that might undo all these preconceived arrangements was, as usual, the weather. Not a forecast was missed on radio, television or in the newspaper; the local weather prophets were consulted and signs from clouds, sea and wind were anxiously interpreted for days beforehand. After all these prognostications were weighed we still did not know what to expect, so the mixed blessing of the fine dry day, though cold and very breezy, which was our lot on that Sunday, 9 June 1974, was accepted with equanimity.

Our intention was to show the president as much of interest as was feasible with the minimum of discomfort and exposure to those chilly draughts from the Atlantic. Arrangements were made to greet the party at the entrance then lead them through a donkey guard of honour to the shop to sign the visitor's book, present the president and his wife with a small gift as a memento of their visit and then, after a long look round, they would join us in the house for refreshments.

People who had agreed to hold donkeys in the guard of honour had a precarious job as a boisterous wind can be infectious to the donkeys, making them behave in a like manner. So much agility and nimbleness of foot was called for, both to get them smartly on parade and to make them keep in ranks. The naughty little foals frisked about in every direction, and decided quite definitely not to pay attention to any authority, either their mothers' or ours! Together as always, and with plenty of attention coming their way from arriving visitors, the twinnies behaved beautifully. Dear old Granny Velvet, the matriarch of our donkey ménage, was warmly wrapped up in a rug, placidly surveying the younger generations. A black mare with teeth worn down to gum level, she walked with short mincing steps as though trying to imitate a child tiptoeing on the pavement stones without touching the dividing lines. Granny's exact age was not known, but from information pieced together it added up to between thirty and forty years with the balance nearer the forties. She was a great favourite with many visitors who will be sad to hear that she has now passed on to a donkey's paradise.

The donkey which really caught all eyes was a tiny broken-coloured filly foal born that very morning to Miss Rockefeller who, though her prefix might suggest otherwise, had been married the previous year to Money Moon. The youngster captured everyone's attention, especially later on when it became known that Mrs Rita Childers, the president's wife, had graciously consented to the foal being called after her in honour of their visit. Not in the guard of honour but ready for inspection near the shop were Shubad saddled and bridled, Alana harnessed to the trap and Ras Shamra to our painted cart, the latter two wearing their best sun hats.

During the exited bustle to get one and all on duty, I was most disconcerted to discover that I had cut my right hand, and although only a tiny wound it was bleeding profusely. Gloveless and handbagless, even on such an auspicious occasion, and wearing cream-coloured apparel without pockets, how was I to avoid either offering a sticky bleeding hand to our president and his wife or to appear besmirched-looking from rubbing a blood-covered paw down the side of my suit? Not a hope of making it to the house and back again before the arrival. In fact there was only just time for my husband, in response to an anguished entreaty, to pass me his white handkerchief which I clutched at tightly to absorb the blood and then jammed back in his pocket, before proffering an only moderately dry, though very welcoming hand to our distinguished guests as they dismounted from their car at the entrance gate.

Accompanied by Col Thomas MacNamara, his ADC, the President of the Republic of Ireland and Mrs Erskine Childers turned their backs to the blustering wind and were led up the driveway between the ranks of our human and donkey friends, as we made the introductions. They seemed genuinely intrigued by their guard of honour, pausing to stroke each donkey, talking with each holder individually while turning to us at intervals to ask questions about the animals. Those donkeys of a chestnut colour were greatly admired. The party were enchanted by the diminutive foal born that morning and as previously mentioned, were happy for the filly to be named Rita in honour of Mrs Childers. They did not forget to pay attention to those saddled and harnessed donkeys who had been patiently awaiting inclusion in the honours. Lastly, we took them into our house where the guests whom they had not already met were introduced, before all were provided with fare to dissipate the chill of the wintry June evening.

All too soon the memorable visit had to come to an end, memorable not only for the compliment paid to us and our donkey farm, but also because Mr and Mrs Childers were such truly delightful personalities with a wide range of enthusiastic interests about which they displayed a warm understanding. When, five months later, the whole country was bereaved by the sudden loss of its president, there were few places outside his home where the death of this fine honourable man, a dedicated servant of Ireland, was more sincerely mourned than here amongst us all.

The wintry weather then continued with only a slight break now and again throughout the whole season. The presidential visit did much to boost public interest in us, both at home and overseas, but nothing could conquer the formidable weather conditions and many holidaymakers departed much earlier than usual. The donkeys too got 'weather depression' and looked as miserable as they felt. No foal pranks like trying to lift ladies' handbags, or pretending to be asleep stretched out in the sun, when really some tummy scratching is desired, are forthcoming on wet days.

We were particularly grateful therefore for our tea-room as luckless families from nearby caravan sites poured into our shelter. The birth of this tea-room was accompanied by some unexpected pangs, due mainly to our total ignorance of certain regulations. Our first modest efforts at catering had proved such a success that, now we were on the coach-tour itineraries, there was no doubt in our minds that we needed a proper tea-room. Surveying our small premises with dismay, we wondered where on earth to find space in which to erect this mini-restaurant. Eventually, after prolonged cogitation, we decided to scrap three stables and reconstruct them as one largish room, next to the shop with a door between them.

The decision once made, no time was lost, and the work was well in hand when a catering inspector drove up. We had met before when making arrangements to sell minerals and ice-creams so I was delighted to tell him that we were now building a tea-room and snack bar as the shop counter from which we sold refreshments previously was not longer viable for the increasing number of visitors. Very politely he then asked to see my caterer's licence. Equally politely, I told him that we did not possess such a thing. The pregnant pause lasted for a few seconds before he informed me that we could be liable for a whopping fine. Completely surprised and rather incensed, I replied that no mention had been made of this at his previous visit. Ah, but then we had only applied for permission to sell minerals and ice-creams . . . ! It seems that once you start to boil water, this constitutes cooking, and cooking requires a special caterer's permit.

Apparently the printed notice at the front gate advertising home-made teas had caught the inspector's eye and drawn him in to see – dare I say it – what was cooking! After apologising for being so misinformed I undertook to apply for a licence immediately, and we entered the room under reconstruction. Here at least four men, including a plumber and an electrician, were all busily at work, carrying out the plans which might now be turned topsy-turvy. Casting an experienced eye over any work completed, the inspector gave an audible sigh, which to me, half expecting more trouble after the setback already suffered, seemed to predict even worse to come. I was vastly heartened then to learn that this had been a sigh of relief: while there were still difficulties ahead, they were nothing to those we might have had, should the work have been too far advanced to allow for the requisite modifications necessary to comply with the catering laws without almost pulling the place to pieces and starting the job over again.

Somewhat cheered by this, I was soon back in the doldrums as the list mounted of all the extra things to do. Every time our friend opened his mouth, he breathed pounds on to our estimate. The men downed tools looking bewildered, but there was no way out, the rules had to be obeyed, so as soon as this guardian of regulations left us, we set about revising our plans in accordance with legal demands, hoping to avoid the hand of the law from another angle – the bankruptcy court! The problem now was whether we could find anywhere suitable for serving food during the coming season. The part of the shop previously devoted to refreshments was already commandeered by the shop, which was badly in need of extra space, and our dining-room was no longer arranged to accommodate the public. The only possible way out was to complete the new stable tea-room, catering regulations and all, so with flogging vigour we tackled the job anew.

Extra timber was required and, thinking to save time in case of a delay in delivery as well as transport expense, we decided to collect it ourselves from the yard some eighteen miles away. Hitching an open donkey-trailer to the car and accompanied by my little dog, I took delivery of the heavy load with a warning from the timber-yard to take it nice and easy on the way home. Nice and easy we went for all of two miles until the car gave a sudden sharp jolt and a loud, clattering noise smote the air. Lurching to a halt and looking round, I discovered the back half of the trailer, plus its two wheels, astride the hedge on the opposite side of the road, while the front half, though still attached to the car, lay twisted on its side, and littered all over the place were sixty planks of timber, 8ft by 1ft. Yes, sixty of those eight by ones; no mistake on that numeration, for were they not carefully counted by the kindly occupants of at least three or four of the multitude of cars, whose owners, for reasons known only to themselves, decided to use this quiet country road on that day.

With the timber laid carefully in a nearby side-road, one of my rescuers unhitched the front of the trailer, while another retrieved the rear end from off the hedge and both were placed near the planks. Thanking those kind helpers, I pulled the car aside to let the world and his wife pass by, while the effusive welcoming licks from my dog did much to conceal my scarlet face. On the drive home my scattered senses returned, and with them the shocking realisation of what might have happened had there been a donkey in the trailer instead of those now thrice-blessed 'eight by ones'. Should we ever buy a second-hand trailer of any kind again, it will not be until after a complete and thorough examination, with special attention to the newly painted areas.

The tea-room gradually began to take shape and soon we were able to furnish it with tables, stools and chairs. A sheaf of unthrashed oats was pilfered from the farm and the heads severed at about 8 or 9in. Stuck carefully along the lower part of a 2in deep length of red sticky tape and attached to the upper edge of the window frame by the top of that tape, these made pelmets which harmonised with the red and beige material of curtains and tablecloths and were in character with the equine surroundings. Harness, photographs and donkey bric-à-brac were destined for the walls, as was a delightful 8ft x 2ft pastoral mural painted on tiles.

The menu took little planning and was to consist of home-made bread, scones, cakes, rhubarb and apple tarts, plus strawberries in season. Butter, jam, cheese and whipped cream would be served as required. There was also tea and coffee as well as our original fare of ice-creams and minerals.

The first couple to take genuine caterer's tea with us did not seem to mind that the tea-room was not quite finished. They came from Pontefract, Yorkshire, where the husband was employed by the English National Coal Board, and were the winners of a competition which gave them a free holiday for two in Ireland. To win the competition they had had to answer six questions about Cambrian Airways and Ireland and, in addition, they had completed a sentence beginning 'I would like an Irish holiday because . . .'. When they came to finishing off the sentence, they tried to include something associated particularly with Ireland and immediately thought of donkeys. Remembering how they had enjoyed an Irish holiday a few years earlier at a town called Bray, the donkey connection seemed too good to miss so they completed the sentence by adding ' . . . we want to hear the donkeys (at) Bray.' This, together with the correct answers to the questions, won them the fortnight's holiday with all expenses paid at a hotel about fifty miles north of here.

Wishing to see the renowned lakes of Killarney which are some distance south of us, and to return the same day, the couple set off early one morning to catch the car-ferry over the Shannon. Passing our gate, they were astonished to see notice of a donkey stud and, moreover, one open to the public. They had no idea that such a place existed and immediately stopped the car, then remembering the unknown road ahead they decided to continue on their way and visit us on the way back. So, in the late afternoon, two tired looking figures walked up our drive and requested tea. When I replied that the tea-room would not be open for a few days they looked so crestfallen that I offered to bring them out some tea from the house, a suggestion which cheered them up immediately. I was surprised when they then asked to see the donkeys for, though refreshed by the tea, they looked as if they had had a long day. It was then that I heard their story, and was able to appreciate their astonishment at coming across a stud devoted solely to the animal intimately connected with their holiday.

Since then the tea-room has brought many more friends of all nationalities. A licence to sell wine is a newly added asset, especially appreciated by continental customers. As we now have limited accommodation available for paying guests, the estimable name of The White Ass Inn has been added to the premises!

That our 'inn' should become as famous as the one so plagiarised is unlikely, but if it can give to the public a fraction of the pleasure which was given by that gay musical play then we will have accomplished something.

We have also established some firm business friendships while stocking the shop. I learnt to accept with equanimity the startled looks from the trade when my only requirement was goods with a donkey image! It is not easy to find suitable items for such a specialised outlet, donkey harness and saddlery having become increasingly hard to obtain. Donkey-orientated souvenirs have to be chased up and down everywhere but, item by item, slowly but surely, we did build up stock with a donkey flavour. This building up also proved difficult as most wholesale firms like to supply goods in large quantities and our shop was too small and too newly established for us to order in bulk, though some large companies were very accommodating and helped by allowing us a small order to start off with. We had, and still have, another difficulty in storing goods; for not only is there little space in the shop but, as it has no central heating, some products would deteriorate very quickly in this seaside climate, so all goods not on display have to be stored in our house.

One of the most popular articles ever sold were our rainbow donkey sweaters, which alas, are now unobtainable. How we came to stock them at all is worth recording. In cold summers or times of illness we sometimes require rugs for the foals, but we failed to find anything suitable on the market, so we decided to seek out available material and have the rugs made in quantity. This was easier said than done. However, after several abortive approaches to firms that deal in horse equipage, we called on our local knitwear factory to see if they had any bright ideas, and found that they had one well worth an experiment. After most of the factory's orders were completed orlon yarn of most colours was left over, and they suggested that if we supplied a template and measurements, donkey rugs of various sizes could be made in a mixture of colours. As it was essential that the rugs were washable, and I knew that orlon garments

Plate 13 Fairview Lady, the first champion donkey at the Royal Dublin Society's Horse Show, 1972, with its owner, Miss Muriel Shackleton. The champion is here enjoying some grass from the Swinfen Perpetual Challenge Trophy presented by the author. The judges were famous sporting artist, Mr Michael Lyne (right) and Mr Richard Stanley *(Irish Times)*

Plate 14 Donkey girl, Sally O'Reilly, sprucing up a youngster *(Limerick Leader)*

Plate 15 (left) Donkeys are proving successful for therapeutic work with sick youngsters. Here Scattery gives a ride to a patient at Our Lady's (psychiatric) Hospital, Enhis, Co Clare *(Noel Barker)*

Plate 16 (below) Enjoying a Christmas 'down-under' is Twill, a miniature broken-coloured stallion exported from Spanish Point *(John Drever)*

launder well, it seemed that this might be the answer to our problem.

Our order was duly completed and delivered, and the rugs made a colourful show in the shop. They were very quickly noticed by about 90 per cent of our customers who, upon asking to see the lovely coloured sweaters, were very disappointed to learn that they were only rugs for our long-eared friends. After explaining many times that we only intended to sell goods relating to donkeys, some bright spark suggested that a donkey owner ought to have a jumper similar to her donkey's rug. Off we went to the same factory to enquire if sweaters could also be made from the offcuts and, after some discussion, it was agreed that they would make them up for us in five different sizes, all to the same pattern as long as we were willing to take whatever colours or mixes were available at the time of the order. Soon our shelves were stocked with rows of rainbow donkey sweaters knitted in thick ribbed orlon, round-necked and long-sleeved, to fit every member of the family from about the age of four upwards, including an outsize. Their beautifully blended colourings, useful design and reasonable price made them a winner and we sold hundreds for three seasons. Oddly enough, some of these sweaters had been made up and sold from the factory before we came on the scene, but it was only when displayed *en masse* in our small shop that the lovely colourings became more of an eye-catcher and the one seemed to sell the other. Sadly, with the introduction of more advanced machinery, these hand-loomed sweaters are no longer profitable to manufacture so we can no longer stock them.

Another very useful attraction is a giant woolly donkey with floppy legs perched up behind the shop counter. He looks so cuddly that many a caller wants to fondle him, which we permit most willingly, especially in bad weather, for it saves numerous tours to our rain-washed fields and shelters to see live though weather-beaten donkeys.

Not having many items of interest to men in the shop, we had made for us some very smart ties with a small donkey motif running through the material. These were slow to sell, mostly being bought by and for donkey owning families; but we were fascinated to note that there was quite a rush on them whenever an American visitor or party came along. When our curiosity broke its bounds, we were most amused to hear that the donkey is the emblem of the US Democratic Party. You can't even keep the donkey out of politics!

7 Our Animal 'Stars'

On arrival, most visitors head for the shop where tickets for tours and rides are available, and where they can browse around, sign the visitors' book, inspect our Friendship Table – holding cards and brochures of our friends all over the country who have hotels, shops or any place of interest which we can recommend personally. Yet they nearly always end up, weather permitting, leaning on the rails of the front paddock. It is here, relaxing awhile and idly looking at the donkeys, that many friendships are forged by our shared interest in these animals. And here we are regaled with many amusing donkey stories both true and fictitious. Several of the donkeys are tied to the railings as they wait, saddled up or harnessed to the vehicles, and it is here that most visitors and donkeys meet each other for the first time.

The small coterie of donkeys kept especially for giving rides to children, for pulling the trap and the painted cart which is decorated in Sicilian style with designs of local interest, are as reliable as it is possible for any animal to be. So far, we are grateful to say, there have been no unpleasant incidents except

OUR ANIMAL 'STARS'

for the odd unbalanced spill which, unless a very small child is involved, brings forth mirth and not dismay! We have recently purchased a rocking-donkey which is installed near the tea-room, so that these very young ones can now rock away for as long as they like, while the parents enjoy their tea, and watch them at the same time. Alana, Rainbow, Ras and Shubad all love their work and the attention they receive. Ras, whose startling manner of giving birth has been described in Chapter 2, was sold to us because she had too fast a trot for carrying the milk churns to the creamery. She can still, after producing many a foal, turn on the speed, and is yet so quiet and gentle when giving rides to children.

An equally favoured, but more unusual member of our asinine family who has been overlooked to date is a three-year-old grey gelding, born of a broken-coloured sire out of a grey dam and named Paddy Medina. Not that anyone can overlook this donkey for long – he literally has an extra pair of 'little legs' upon which to stand up for himself! A snap-shot of him as a foal sent to us by Mrs Kathleen Whitford, who bred and now wished to sell him, clearly showed these additional 'legs' and aroused our interest so much that we decided to see this foal for ourselves; so with Georgina, one of our assistants, I made the long journey to Kilkenny. In reality the little fellow's remarkable appendages looked even more intriguing than in the photograph, and in no time at all we had bought him, arranged for him to be gelded while still with his dam, and be delivered to us when weaned before the end of the year.

Paddy Medina's extra legs, complete with hooves, are attached to the inner side of both his natural forelegs, though happily proving no hindrance to his freedom of movement. Is there any explanation in nature for their presence or are they just deformities? Are there any recorded instances of similar extra legs on other donkeys? Browsing through the limited literature on *Equus asinus* I found no recorded instance of anything like this but, as the evolution of the ass would appear to be similar to that of the horse, my mind went back to the early history of the horse millions of years ago, when the ancestors of our present-day equines had on their feet, instead of a single solid hoof, four toes on the forefeet and three on the hindfeet, each ending in a separate hoof, the third toe being the largest and longest. Behind these toes was a flexible but tough pad or cushion. Over millions of years the outer toe of the foreleg disappeared and, for many more millions of years the animal remained three-toed, until eventually, over the ages, the side toes too were lost and the horse and its existing relatives became single-toed as they remain today.

Fig 1
View of Paddy Medina's extra legs

We are told that the outermost toe on the front legs of the four-toed horse disappeared and left only a non-functioning vestige of it. The then remaining outer toes shrunk upwards and inwards into what are now called splint bones and were entirely concealed beneath the skin of the leg, while the middle toe increased in length and breadth.

I was most interested to find that there have been well authenticated instances of horses with a protuberance on their forelegs. To quote Captain Hayes's *Points of the Horse:*

We occasionally find in the horse that one or both of the splint bones are provided, like the cannon bone (the main foreleg bone), with a more or less perfect pastern and hoof . . . Apparently these abnormal digits are not monstrosities, like the sixth finger or toe which is sometimes found on the hand or foot of a human being, but are reversion to a former type.

Similarly, George Gaylord Simpson, the distinguished scientist, author and friend of Teilhard de Chardin, states in his book *Horses* that 'Traces of the ancient side toes still occur in horse embryos.' In the preface to the 1961 paperback issue of that book he also adds the following interesting comment on the use of these extra toes:

> Shotwell further concludes that the small side toes of the three-toed grazers not only served as stops or buffers, as suggested in this book, but also were functional in improving the footing for sudden evasive action in the particular environment of those horses. The fascinating connection between evolutionary changes and ways of life is thus further exemplified.

The hooves on Paddy Medina's extra toes almost touch the ground at times and have to be pared like his others. They are similar in shape and texture to the large front hooves but are without the frog. We have had both forelegs X-rayed but I doubt if the results will be available before this book is published. Incidentally, Paddy's dam has had another foal since his birth and this one is quite normal.

Another strange-looking donkey in the stud is the stallion Shron Dubh – Gaelic for Black Snout. True to his appellation that is just what he has, well as many other definite black markings on a grey-background coat. Each time I look at him, I am puzzled; with a little extra marking he could be a zebra, yet other markings indicate that he could be a wild ass. Only one thing is certain, and that is he is not at all like the ordinary grey domestic ass.

Unique as some of our donkeys are they do not take precedence over the other members of our animal family. Indeed, one of the inmates who claims a large majority of our attention, and seems to think that he merits even more, is the Horrible Dog, alias Teddy, Mr Edward, Teddy Swinfen, Edward Dog and other names that are unmentionable. He is the most abominably noisy, untrainable, disobedient and obstreperous dog of doubtful ancestry that I have ever known – but one toothy grin of apology from him and you are lost, and the threatening kick you had been withholding for all of the last five minutes, but which you were sure you would not hesitate to aim in his direction when a visitor was not looking, still clings to your foot. You just cannot win with that dog. As fast as he provokes you to a bad humour with his vociferous barking, he charms you again with his ludicrous smile – no worry to him that you have a chronic sore throat trying to admonish him.

In that dog's own estimation he is undisputed canine king of the area, his despotic rule not even allowing another of the same race to go by on the main road without a dash down the avenue in case the traveller should dare advance into his territory. In his younger days – he is now eleven years old – there was many a time when this battle-scarred black and white, well, let's say it, collie, lay curled up in his basket in the hall, sleeping off the painful results of meeting rivals on his courting adventures. He visits almost every house in the neighbourhood to gather booty and there is nothing going on that he doesn't know about or have his paw in. The donkeys all love him and, when in the mood they play together, though should Mr Edward get too curious about a very new foal he is smartly warned to mind his own business. The visitors love him too, once they have braved that outrageous barking which is mostly a portrayal of the sheer excitement of living. His other bark, brought forth when strangers come to the door, a postman appears, or things go bump in the night, has a completely different tone and means business. How does he hear the postman coming up the road on his bicycle before we have even seen him, or know the difference between our visitors and the stranger at the door? You tell me!

Having reigned supreme in our household since my little grey poodle departed this life several years ago, we dreaded what

OUR ANIMAL 'STARS'

Horrible Dog's reaction might be to the arrival of the two Colourpoint long-hair cats (Himalayans to Americans) which were soon to join our family. His relationship to neighbouring cats was only as close as they would allow him to get when at a full-speed retreat. When Mister Ister and Bungie arrived, Edward Dog was relaxing in his basket in the hall, leashed to a nearby radiator. He simply glanced up as these two bundles of long honey-coloured fur with dark-brown ears, paws and tail, the latter resembling a fox's brush, were lowered to the ground at a safe distance from him. Then, hearing some kittenish miaows he shot out of his basket to see two pairs of startled china-blue eyes looking at him, before their owners sped upstairs out of sight. Knowing the dog was safely anchored we left all three alone to get acquainted in their own way, only keeping a watchful eye in the background and, when unleashing Teddy, making sure he was locked outside and the cats safely inside. The excitement only lasted a few days before they all became buddies and in no time at all Mister Ister had taken over Teddy's basket, with Teddy permitted in sometimes, but more often relegated to the doormat alongside.

On the whole, cats are more acceptable than dogs as companions to donkeys. Except in voice, the donkey is of a calm, placid nature and is less likely to be upset by the quiet stealthy movements of a cat than by the more noisy movements of a dog. From the beginning our donkeys and cats took to each other and the latter spend many hours of the day perched on the concrete railings watching the inhabitants of the paddock. Should a soft, asinine muzzle get too forward, a gentle smack soon sends it backwards. Mister Ister, like the Horrible Dog, must also have a paw in every pie. He follows me down the paddock to see the donkeys, into the stables and, worst of all, creeps under visitors' cars; could it be that we are in for a Horrible Cat?

Other animals viewed from our windows and only honorary members of the family, are two hares. One day last March I watched them closely through binoculars for a long time. The paddock was having its winter rest and was without donkeys, so these two large hares, squatting about a yard apart, were left undisturbed. The weather was cold with the wind, though not strong, coming from the east, as is usual here at this time of year, and was obviously not conducive to March Hare frolics, though there is no doubt that they were getting their personal spring-cleaning done in good time for the occasion, when it arose. Watching them intently, I was struck by certain similarities to both donkeys and cats. Their long agouti-coloured black-edged ears with the light-coloured linings looked, in their flexibility, like twins to those of a foal when disturbed by something and, fearing discovery, they also would crouch down and drop their ears below spine level to appear unnoticed. Their eyes too are set like a donkey's and, when relaxed, take on that same almond shape.

It is in the hares' method of grooming that I see a resemblance to the cat. The long hind legs came in for a lot of concentrated attention, and what a long length they are when fully stretched out, cat-like. Their muzzles too are very active and the animals look so bright and intelligent when they sit upright and gaze about. On this particular occasion one had just got up and attempted to rub noses with the other but, getting a rebuff, was about to squat down again, when the Horrible Dog espied him and gave the poor railings a belt of his hind legs as he flashed through in pursuit. As there is not a chance that he will get near them, I do not worry, only hope and pray that the species will not suffer complete annihilation, and that the hares' pitiful dying screams on the coursing field will soon be a shameful memory as greyhounds seek to win more honourable rewards.

Edward Dog's passage through the railings did, however, disturb the jackdaws which perch there from morning till night, squabbling away, and up to all kinds of mischief. Hardly waiting until the donkeys have finished their feed, the jackdaws jump into the bowls and troughs to get their peck of grain. Not content with that, they often make flying visits to the donkeys themselves, which last far longer than the term suggests. Landing on the donkeys' backs, the birds travel up and down, pecking off large wads of hair with which to line their nests, before returning for more. I have seen as many as five or six birds on one donkey, and once I saw two of them each perched on an ear! The donkeys do not seem to mind this activity in moderation and if the jackdaws get too persistent, they are soon driven off. I have even seen the foals play games by chasing them and, though the birds hop quickly away, the foal keeps on pursuing them. I gather that it is a different story with magpies, as their peck is more severe, causing wounds and sores.

Perhaps lack of restraint on the part of the magpie is prompted by the same feelings as those of the blue-tit referred to by Aelian (a Roman of the second century who wrote in Greek), who states in one of his books on animals that: 'The bitterest hate exists between the Blue Tit and the Ass, for directly the Ass brays the Blue Tit's eggs are smashed . . . And so to avenge its offspring the Blue Tit leaps upon the Ass's sore places and feeds on them.'

Observations on donkeys and their ways are happily not confined to second-century Romans. One visitor to the stud, Mr J. P. Murray after leaning on the rails for some time gazing intently at the occupants of the paddock wanted to know, then and there, why some of our donkeys did not have crosses on their backs. Gathering my wits together I explained that, in my opinion, our donkeys today were descendants of more than one species of wild ass, and as some of these wild asses did not have the cross stripe over their shoulders it was therefore lacking in some of ours. I also stated my belief that the donkeys' horizontal leg stripes appeared or not also by reason of this wild mixed ancestry. Later, after the conformation points of the donkey had been drawn up by our newly formed Irish Donkey Society, this anxious visitor sent me the following ditty:

> Where Are All The Crosses Gone?
>
> While the people of Ireland are brave men and good
> And quite unaccustomed to theft
> Some asses that brood in the Spanish Point Stud
> of crosses their backs are bereft
> There's a thief in the joint in old Spanish Point
> the evidence can plainly be seen

OUR ANIMAL 'STARS'

> For alack and alas from the back of each ass
> The cross has been taken quite clean
> The devil we are told by philosophers of old
> Had evil that none could surpass
> A criminal so sly would take the sight from your eye
> or the cross from the back of an ass
> Tho' it says in the Book the good Lord Himself took
> A ride on an ass with propriety
> He did not imprint it says the little book printed
> By the Irish Donkey Society.

Such correspondence is the joy of our lives, though answering it all can prove a bane at times. We love hearing from visitors, some of whom send along photographs of their visit, while others enclose newspaper cuttings, stories, poems and any other donkey material to hand. Several people write to ask advice on a problem they have with a donkey, thinking we might have had similar trouble. We have a veritable treasure-chest of letters, but not all of them answered – yet! Perhaps the plum is an answer to an advertisement we inserted in our local newspaper *The Clare Champion* in October 1964 for a 'Young, dark coloured donkey mare'. Here it is:

> Dear Sir,
>   I seen your ad in the Champion today
> I got a good ass and I think
> shes in fole too and she has
> black ears and whats left of
> her tale that the ponys after leaving
> to her bad cess to him is black.
> You could say she was a dark
> ass alright but a bit ruff but if
> she ruff shes right too and she
> has a grand bawl that youd
> here in America.
> Id say she was in fole alright
> my missus sais she is and she shoud
> know as shes buryed
> 6 young children God rest there

soles and I wasnt ther when it
happened but she told me
it was alright.
Shes a aged ass as she was
droped the very day my 4th
girl was and shes in America this
long time but strong.
Dont pay any etenshun to
the tinkers mark that does
be on her they done it on me
when I had a drink taken.
Im askin £17–10s seventeen
tin for the ass but would
take less. Make me
an offer.
Hoping you will call
     I remain yours truly
      sined Tim Carty
      Ennis Co Clare

To my everlasting regret I must confess that we never called on him. We picked up this letter with other replies on the way to a hospital, nearly 200 miles distant. On our return some time later such an accumulation of matters awaited us, as well as offers of younger asses to view, that it was quite a while before this masterpiece came to our attention once more. From nearby friends, we found some who knew the writer, and perhaps I will be able to visit him yet, though I doubt to find the aged ass still there.

 Another delightful note came from a man in the midlands who had a certain coloured ass which I required. Having previously driven all over the country on many a wild goose chase, I wrote to say that he lived too far away for me to go there and back in a day. His reply contains a long description of the ass, which he obviously thought was a beauty (as she was), then, without any punctuation he goes on 'you could stay with my sister nearby' and, his mind returning immediately to his beloved ass, he continued 'but she's not in foal this year'. This

OUR ANIMAL 'STARS'

time we did call, purchased the ass and made a lifetime friendship with the vendor.

The origin of Paddy Medina's legs, the stallion with the strange colouring, donkeys without crosses on their backs and letters in English-Irish, all make this chapter seem full of if's and but's, how's and why's, when's and wherefore's. To round off in suitable vein, I hope the answers will not prove as unexpected as that received by the toff walking in the country. On meeting a local with his ass and cart, the man airily enquired if that contraption would take him to the city, only to be told, 'I'm not sure sir, as I doubt if the harness would fit ye'!

8   On With the Show

By 1970, it was clear that the donkey was attracting attention all over the country. Several counties were including donkey classes in their agricultural shows, and I felt it was time to form a society in which this growing enthusiasm could find a focal point and gather strength. A friend, Mrs Murray Mitchell, agreed to help and we put an advertisement in the press inviting anyone interested in such a venture to write to us. This brought an excellent response and led us to arrange a public meeting at which the Irish Donkey Society was born with Mrs Mitchell and myself voted in as vice-president and president respectively, the other offices being filled by equally enthusiastic members. It was exciting to see so great a regard for this animal by such a large cross-section of people, gathered together from all over the country and who, for centuries, had chiefly looked upon it as a beast of burden.

The main aims of our society were to raise the status of the donkey and to stamp out cruelty and ill-treatment. It would also act as a governing body to whom show committees would refer for guidance in drawing up rules for donkey classes, authorise a panel of judges, publish a specification indicating the desirable conformation of the various types of donkeys and later form a register. An early wish, which unhappily fell by the wayside after a time, was that general meetings, scheduled well in advance, should take place in each county in turn to give small owners, especially those living off the beaten track and unable to travel far, the opportunity to participate more closely in the society's affairs. My reason for suggesting them came from the belief that they would encourage more active co-operation between those members whose donkeys are still in active service around country districts, as is the case all along the western side of Ireland, and the owners of donkeys in the populous and more easily accessible areas.

For nearly four years I kept pace with the society and edited the three issues of its yearly magazine *Assile*. Having taken leave of absence in order to write this book, I doubt if I shall take up office again. Our business here has expanded enormously and requires all the time we can give it. This, coupled with the onerous task of dealing with all the correspondence my life with the society entailed, and on top of the correspondence my donkey interests entail anyway, plus other private factors, virtually prohibits it. Nevertheless, the Irish Donkey Society is a child of my heart and will always retain my interest and good wishes.

Once established, the society went from strength to strength, though suffering the odd teething troubles which beset most newly formed organisations. With donkeys now regularly exhibited at most agricultural shows we aspired to even greater heights for our protégé – nothing less than admission to the Royal Dublin Society's world famous Horse Show would satisfy us. For some years past I had cherished hopes of realising this ambition for the donkey, but not until we had formed a society with its own rules and regulations, listed the conformation points upon which it wished the animals to be judged (eventually settled by a majority vote from a list of points put forward for consideration), and selected a panel of judges, would the RDS consider this request. With all this accomplished, the application was renewed and the reply eagerly awaited. After due consideration by the committee, back came the joyous news that it 'agreed to having Donkey Classes at forthcoming Horse Shows starting this year'. We were jubilant. Not a moment was lost in preparing for the big day, the day that would see the Irish ass/donkey, for so long looked upon here as the poorer man's horse, for the first time, join the élite of the domestic animal world on show in Dublin.

By the afternoon of 13 August 1972, the ninety-six entries for the eight donkey classes were gathered on the showground at Ballsbridge; surely a first-time entry to be proud of by any standards. As the day wore on, excited owners and an enthusiastic public watched the two judges, Michael Lyne, the well-known English artist, and Richard Stanley, Chairman of our Society, cope splendidly with their duties. The first entrant to win a class for donkeys at this event was Mr John McCartney's fine piebald stallion, King Jacko. The last class of the day, confined to animals placed first and second in previous classes, was won by Miss Muriel Shackleton's lovely beige/grey mare, Fairview Lady, which thus became the first Champion Donkey at the Dublin Horse Show. Judging by the comments of the onlookers and the delight of the children who fondled the animals, especially the foals, whenever possible, I think we can say that the donkeys' Dublin début was an unqualified success.

We were very grateful to the show officials, in particular to those in the ring who took tremendous pains with us newcomers, and to David Gray, who guided both donkey and owner along the intricate pathway to the ring. Our obligations to John E. Wylie, Secretary of the Executive Committee, are many, for he was our channel of communication with the RDS from the beginning and his constant help had been deeply appreciated, as has that of his assistant, Mrs Scott.

It is the general policy of the RDS to have overseas judges for the August show, but for our first-time attendance it was agreed that we could divide the honours. We had to look overseas, however, for the next season's judges. For some years I have been a member of two American donkey societies, have donkeys registered with them, and have enjoyed a lively correspondence with their members. This gave me the idea that we should invite their presidents to visit our country – and in what better capacity than as judges for the 1973 Dublin Show donkey classes. Both presidents were delighted at the invitations and decided to bring along their wives. Carl A. Wilson II of Indiana, President of the American Donkey and Mule Society, even decided to spend some time seeing the countryside and our rural life with his family, before going on to Dublin. Fortunately, near us at Lahinch, virtually on the sea as they wished, is the excellent Aberdeen Arms Hotel, which served this delightful family as a comfortable headquarters where they were later joined by David J. Parker, President of the American Council of Spotted Asses, and his wife, from Montana. This engaging couple had the misfortune to lose their luggage on the trip over. As they arrived only a few days before the show David Parker appeared in the show ring wearing the clothes in which he had left home, complete with ten-gallon Stetson hat! Everywhere he went there were offers to buy the hat from him, and I'm delighted to report that it now hangs in our tea-room, a much prized gift, kindly sent to us by its owner on his return home.

Up to that time 1973 had been a disordered year for us with both my mother and husband, Carol, hospitalised. Carol remained in hospital nearly 200 miles away until April, shortly before we were due to open the stud to the public at Easter. This allowed us little time for pre-season preparations, such as hiring extra staff and purchasing goods for the shop and the ingredients for our catering. Unable to obtain a cook-cum-waitress at such short notice, I spent the remainder of the season in the kitchen, belligerently flourishing the rolling pin, whipping up the cakes and cutting out as scones or shortcake a donkey's head with sliced raisins as eyes and nostrils, the latest addition to our menu, billed as 'long-eared buns'. Sporadically serving in the tea-room and shop, picking baskets of strawberries, making up 'surprise packets', foal watching and many other necessary jobs – ably assisted by some young staff – kept us ever on the go. As my husband and mother recovered, they joined us at the front.

The height of our season comes in August so it was impossible for me to leave the business and accompany our American friends to Dublin. Nevertheless, my husband, taking advantage of a pre-arranged check-up at the hospital, managed to get to the show to see these knowledgeable and efficient judges engrossed in their work. And, as the following extract from a letter John E. Wylie wrote to me, as President of the Irish Donkey Society, after the show, reveals, the donkeys are at Dublin to stay: 'We have had nothing but praise for the Donkey Classes and they have now established themselves as one of the features and "crowd-pullers" . . . We were especially pleased this year to welcome the American Judges who lent an added international atmosphere to the judging.' The next year's judges came from England.

I am often asked why I do not participate in the show ring, either by showing my donkeys or acting as judge. The simple reply is that, living as we do on the mid-west coast, nearly every show ring is a long way from us and, with all our visitors during the summer season, we have neither sufficient time nor labour to take part in shows as well, the exception, of course, being our local county show in Ennis. Another reply is that where animals are concerned, my more personal interests in them lie in other directions. When in days gone by horses were part of my life, my interests lay mostly in their use for hunting, point-to-pointing and racing and in a non-spectacular manner I was able to indulge in all these activities. Had I then had the opportunity of owning a stud farm and breeding horses, that would have become my main interest, but I was only able to look at and enjoy other people's studs, for I never owned more than the occasional brood mare. My horses and I never made the show ring together, purely because my personal interest in them was elsewhere, as it is now in donkeys.

A further reason for our not showing is that my absorption in donkeys encompasses all sorts and kinds of their breed, and their potential in any direction, so their presence in the show ring is only part of my general interest, rather than my particular one. Acting as a judge would also pose many a problem for me because, rightly or wrongly, I find myself at variance with some of the points of conformation set up by the donkey societies both here and across the channel. It is better then to air my views out of the ring and, should it seem a little recreant to do so here, those who hold different views need only feel affronted privately, not publicly as in the show ring. With the exception of the extremities of ears, tail and hooves, the donkey is, I feel, too often judged by its resemblance to a good-looking pony or horse, and this is where our judgement goes astray. Also besides these conformation points which, in my opinion, are different, there are others of which we have too little knowledge as yet for us to lay down strict rules.

That there must be a set of rules by which to judge a donkey in shows is without question, but until we have our donkeys sorted out into groups according to their uses and capabilities and their suitability for particular purposes, I feel we should not have too many hard and fast rules, other than the important one of good constitutional health, before allowing them to be entered into a stud book. Better still, let us stick to registration only for the time being. The donkey has the ability to participate in many useful and entertaining lines of occupation, but the manner in which he is formed will not be the best for every pursuit. For example, the qualities sought after for draught purposes are not the ones best suited to a pack-animal or a riding donkey. If, as we hope, the donkey is here to stay, he ought to be encouraged in his particular sphere, and his owners must not be made to feel that their pet is redundant because he has been culled from a stud book which might look, at this early stage in its life, as though it was only interested in Mr, Mrs or Miss World beauty contestants. Insomuch as his nearest relatives, *Equus caballus*, have separate 'who's who' for their individual species, so should we aim at separation for *Equus asinus*. I firmly believe this means that a classification and identification of our donkeys is more necessary than a one-class recognition with all its limitations.

In 1971, when gathering information for a paper on the conformation points of the donkey, on which the Irish Donkey

Society were to vote to assess the future desired shape and condition of their animals, I drew special attention to three parts of the anatomy: jaws, quarters and limbs. While stating that I considered these features to be different from the corresponding ones in the horse, I was unable to give my authoritative reasons for such conjecture. Nor am I able to do so here, but I can at least give some justification for these ideas.

At one show in the summer of 1970, an excellent judge of horses first drew my attention to parrot-mouth (upper teeth over-lapping the lower owing to the shape of the jaw) in donkeys. The animal in question was a handsome colt foal which undoubtedly would have been among the prize winners without this so-called blemish. My interest was instantly aroused as I'd often observed this tendency to parrot-mouth in many donkeys, but had not considered it further. Once I stopped to think about it, I was surprised to discover just how many times I had noticed parrot-mouths, especially in foals.

I personally have only had time to do a little research into the subject, but have found enough information to encourage me to keep on searching. For instance, in the examination by archaeologists of ancient tombs in the Middle East, it has been noted that the curve of the lower jaw-bones of asses found in these graves was greater than that of horses, and the experts also remarked upon the extreme variability of the angle of turn-up in these lower jaw-bones. This leads me to wonder whether our parrot-mouth is really a defect – unless, of course, it is exceedingly pronounced – or whether it may not be just a natural-characteristic legacy from the past. Donkeys are not exclusively grazers by nature but are also browsers, requiring coarse grasses and other rough foods, with which their large intestines can cope to the betterment of their well-being. So far too I have found no evidence that parrot-mouthed donkeys are bad doers.

From my paper of suggestions from which the conformation points were to be chosen, I quote the following remarks pertaining to the quarters and limbs.

> Strong rounded quarters seem to be 'the thing' for our handsome donkey to

possess. But in describing an Asiatic wild ass whose natural abode was in a mountainous area it was said, 'its hind-quarters are much more developed in length and strength' (ie more than the wild asses who lived on the plains). I have noticed that various donkeys have a tendency to drooping and pointed quarters, this could be due to the 'more upright pelvis' before the muscles of the quarters have had time or opportunity to develop. This point of conformation together with the 'hind legs well under him' is not frowned upon by the owners of horses for hunting, as it makes for more agility in jumping, though not for speed. As neither jumping nor speed are the main requisites for our donkeys in the show ring, do we object to this tendency to drooping and pointed quarters?

I believe that like their African cousins the zebras, some asses show a legacy of the past in having their hind legs much more 'under them' than the horse; the reason being that their pelvis is more upright, aiding them to make a quick rotatory movement when attacked by their enemies.

Once again I have had little time to spend on the study of these matters. Nevertheless, while in correspondence with Mrs Daphne Kingsley-Lewis, I discovered that she held many opinions similar to my own on the shape of the donkey's quarters and she has kindly given me leave to quote the following from her paper entitled 'Skeletal Structure of the Donkey compared with the Horse':

The 'championship factor' for donkey stallions – a round rump – is *not* normal to the donkey, especially the male donkey; it is produced by 'Crush gelding', the feeding of hormone-additive meals designed to fatten male piglets (especially in the region of the hams), or by the administration of female hormones by injections to the same end. If this is known to and understood by judges, these round rump donkeys would go further down the line – which would intend to discourage such practices.

The more a donkey is muscled-up, the more angular it will appear when viewed from the rear, due partly to the fact that the processes on the vertebrae are, in the donkey, longer in proportion to the size of the vertebrae than is the case with the horse or pony, and partly to the fact that the pelvis of the donkey differs from that of the horse in shape and proportion. The 'set-on' of the leg to the pelvis at the hip joint is also slightly different in the donkey, but it is the minor difference between the horse and the donkey tail bones – the vertebrae behind the sacrum – which, in fact, cause the greatest

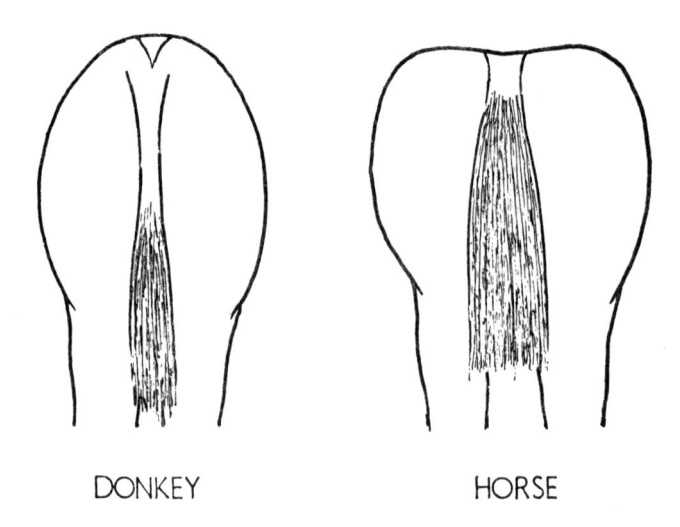

Fig 2 Rear view of donkey and horse to show difference in silhouette caused by prominent spinal processes of donkey and by differences in proportions and tilt of pelvic bones

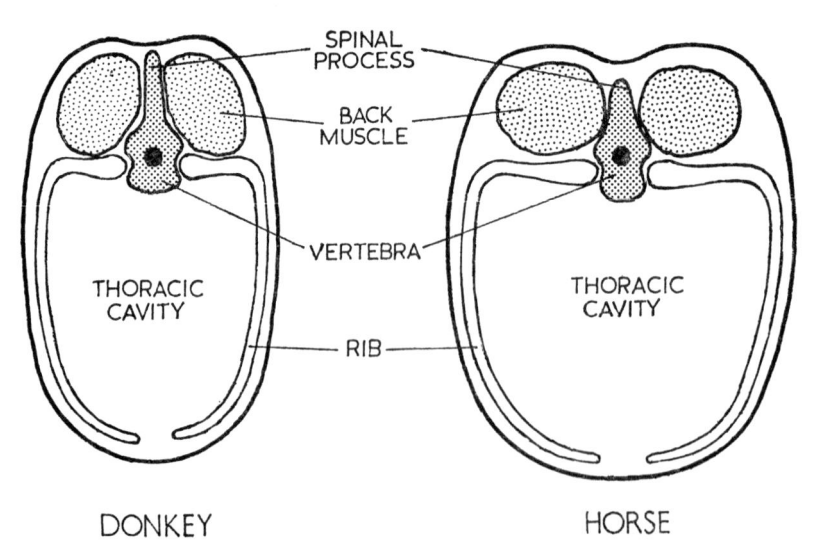

Fig 3 Diagrammatic representation of section through ribcages of donkey and horse illustrating different proportion of vertebrae and ribs – much simplified and not to scale

difference in the silhouette seen from the rear. The donkey retains far more of a hint of the process on the upper tail bones giving the silhouette a somewhat 'tented' appearance.

The diagrams are intended to show the difference in shape caused by the difference in the springing of the ribs in the horse and donkey, allied to the difference in length of the processes upon the vertebrae which, in turn, have an effect upon the back muscles; the horse is altogether more rounded in form and, due to the structural mechanics of its skeleton, the horse perforce has a weaker back than the donkey.

A donkey with a body resembling that of a horse is a *weak* donkey and a *poor* specimen of its species. If we encourage the breeding of such donkeys we will take away the natural strength of the race and we will be adding *nothing* to compensate for the lack of strength. This statement has a sound basis in engineering principles, it is a matter of simple geometry and strength of structures, as can be seen from the diagram below where the cross-sectional shape of the horse and donkey rib cages have been represented in outline as ellipses.

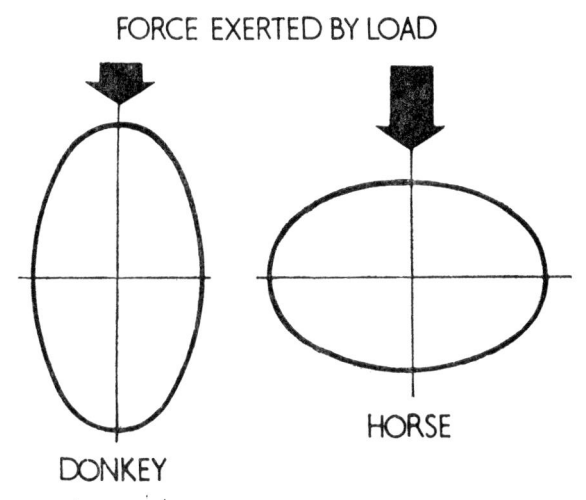

Fig 4   The donkey is represented as an ellipse with its *longer* axis vertical while the horse is represented as an ellipse with its *shorter* axis vertical, thus showing the relationship of their respective body forms

It is easy to find in books on structural engineering, references to the fact that a far greater force is needed to deform an ellipse through its longer axis than is needed to deform the structure through its shorter axis. This demonstrates that the great strength and weight-carrying ability of the donkey is due to its bone structure, which gives it size for size, and weight for weight, an advantage over the horse; it can be said to follow from this that a donkey with a 'horse back' is not a good but a poor type of donkey. A relatively small donkey can safely carry a weight which would require quite a big horse to support it safely, and therein lies the *natural* virtue of the donkey when considering its usefulness to man.

If we are to devise and impose a new artificial conformation (as present day judging would lead one to surmise) then we must think very carefully indeed about the problems which will, in time, arise from our actions, problems such as the 'slipped discs' suffered by the new, 'improved' dachsunds, will seem nothing compared with the difficulties which we will make for ourselves – to say nothing of the unnecessary suffering of pain and discomfort caused to the unfortunate donkey.

The suggestions concerning the limbs which I put forward for the Irish Donkey Society to consider and vote on were:

Forelegs should be straight and squarely placed when viewed from the front, suggesting a perpendicular line from point of shoulder to ground which should bisect the knee, cannon (bone between knee and fetlock), pastern and hoof. When viewed from the side, a perpendicular line from the centre of the shoulder joint should meet the ground at the centre of the hoof. The limbs should be clean and flat with back sinews standing well out. Knees should be flat and broad and showing good bone throughout; pasterns longish on forelegs and rather upright on hind legs.

Hocks should be well-defined, neither too bow-shaped when viewed from the side (sickle-hocked), nor too turned-in when viewed from the back (cow-hocked): gaskins broad and well-muscled. A matter of interest here is that, although severely frowned upon in the horse world, cow-hocks are relatively common among donkeys and mules, with apparently no impediment to their performance, not rendering them more than ordinarily liable to throw out bony growths or to suffer from strains of tendons or ligaments.

Some other random comments on the form of *Equus asinus*, either wild or domestic, may be of interest. In 1825 Reginald Heber, Bishop of Calcutta, noted that in the park of the governor's country residence he saw an ass from the Cape of Good Hope of which he wrote: 'It is extremely strong and *bony*, of beautiful form, has a fine eye and good countenance.' Also in 1825, an Encyclopaedia of Agriculture observes of the domestic ass: 'It is due also to the unbending lines of the spine that his motions are rendered so uneasy to a person placed on the middle of his back.'

A mid-nineteenth-century naturalist describing the wild asinine group, states that '*the croup is narrow*, and often more elevated than the withers', and of the domestic ass he says that 'no domestic animal, in proportion to its bulk, can carry a greater weight'.

When describing two breeds of West African asses, H. Epstein mentions that one breed has a 'short croup' and the other a 'straight back, only slightly sloping croup'. He continues, when writing about the asses from the Atlas Countries, that according to Vaysse (1952) the Moroccan asses are nearly always cow-hocked, but extremely hardy.

Before we hand down our conformation rules to those who come after us, we should perhaps remember that the study of present-day donkeys is not yet very advanced, and now is the time to decide the particular uses for which we require them and what conformations would be most desirable for those disparate uses. It might mean that certain points which would be considered desirable in donkeys bred for some purposes would yet be regarded as defects in donkeys intended for other uses. For example, a breed of wild ass which seldom lived at a lower altitude than 10,000ft had a pronounced convexed-nosed appearance, and I understand that this shape helped facilitate its breathing at such heights by providing room for large nasal passages. This Roman-nosed effect may have its uses in such regions, but it would appear to be superfluous here and, being to us an unattractive conformation point, it seems that we could safely breed it out.

The blending and intermingling of peoples has sometimes created new nations, and it is the same with animals; not that new species have been created but, in some instances, the old breeds have been modified to such an extent as to make it appear incredible that their descendants have come from the original stock. Scientists adhere closely to anatomical significations in their determination of lines of ancestral descent. I feel sure that, when in due course all available evidence is sieved and weighed by the experts, they will find our present-day ass is descended from a mixture of both the African and Asiatic breeds of wild ass. I say this, despite the fact that I know of no recorded instances of fertile hybridisation between the wild asses. In searching through such books on mammalian hybrids as I can find, I am struck by the negative nature of so much of the evidence. So many possible hybrids are either 'presumed' to be infertile or else recorded as 'probably' sterile. Much of the evidence is based on experimental matings carried out in zoos, and many wild animals do not readily mate in captivity. I am only a layman in such matters and, for me, such lack of proof is not strong enough to refute the evidence of the physical appearance, colouring and conformation of many of our present-day donkeys.

9 Outward Bound

The question that slips involuntarily from many a lip when discussing donkeys is that evergreen enquiry, 'do they pay?' It's a perfectly legitimate query; nevertheless, realising that it calls for an answer in monetary terms, you feel a slight antipathy towards the questioner for even suggesting that you might look on your friends, four-legged and long-eared though they be, as worth only pounds and pence. You think of the companionable days you have spent with the donkeys and marvel anew at the mysterious bond of affection that can exist between man and beast once their confidence has been won – an affection that has nothing to do with cupboard love and, with the exception of the instinctive maternal love possessed by them, exceeds in devotion any love they have for each other. You recall the lovely summer evenings with them in the fields along by the sea when, almost mesmerised by the waves as they roll in with a seeming monotony yet are never the same, and by those contented sounds of rythmic munching, you are lulled into tranquility. Musing, you remember bonds of unity: 'in sickness and in health, for better, for worse, for richer, for poorer' until 'with all my worldly goods I thee endow' brings you to an abrupt halt and, as though sensing your thoughts, a furry figure approaches with a tender jostle to remind you of your responsibilities.

But, to reply to the question in purely monetary terms, in our early days, yes, the donkeys did pay. The publicity given to our venture helped to awaken many a person who, like us, had been asleep for so long with regard to the potential of *Equus asinus* for the general public. And I must say that the donkeys have had a wonderful 'press' in Ireland. If any of the newspapers have treated them with ridicule, I have no knowledge of it; with fun at times, maybe – for our enjoyment and no doubt for the donkeys also, could they but read. But here a private word to that lively reporter who tied the word 'psychedelic', even with a question mark attached, to a donkey of ours. Next time he comes to call he had better have a fund of smart answers ready for the public when we propel him on a conducted tour!

Once public interest was aroused, many of those who were in a position to do so decided to go in for donkeys and, as the broken-coloured ones were greatly in the minority, these were much more sought after and more costly. At that time we had both a piebald and a skewbald (broken-coloured) stallion which we advertised for stud purposes at a stated service fee. Owners came to us from all over the country with plain-coloured mares to mate with these stallions in the hope that they would throw broken-coloured (or 'battys' as they are called locally) foals. Remuneration from the stud fees made it very worthwhile in those early years, but I knew this could not continue *ad lib* because geographically we are situated out on a limb, only easily accessible from the north and east, as crossing the Shannon car-ferry from the south would simply add to the owners' expenses. As time went on and the interest in donkeys grew, more conveniently sited stallions were advertised for service and so lessened the call upon ours.

This was a happy state of affairs, for here was a situation that would act as a lever to raise the value of donkeys in general, and thus enable an owner to breed a donkey and care for it well, safe in the knowledge that if he later wished to sell, he would have a marketable proposition. After all, traders know their costs and make their own market in nearly every commodity, except possibly in times of unusual scarcity and abundance, and if their goods are not subject to outside control, their price will be expected to fluctuate like other merchandise.

The donkey trade so far has followed an understandable, if not entirely desirable course. Unhappily there are always people on the look-out for get-rich-quick schemes without carefully studying what is entailed beforehand and the donkey was not overlooked in this sphere. So, when news of the high prices being paid for broken-coloured stock gradually became known, many speculators bought up as many donkeys as they could find very cheaply, merely for financial reasons, hoping to breed highly priced stock from them when mated to broken-coloured stallions but overlooking the cost of the keep, care and attention necessary until the foals were ready for sale. When they realised that the quick riches were imaginary, such people sold out as rapidly as they could, to look for easier profits elsewhere. This unsettled the market, but left the donkeys in stronger hands for the future, because their owners would now be only those who wished to keep the animals for other purposes than purely making money. It is now up to those who know what it costs to keep donkeys to place a realistic price on them, and not bring the donkey back to square one by undervaluing him.

Many of the get-rich-quick fraternity went from donkeys to cattle, which appeared to be an 'odds on' bet. But when it became clear that this scheme was not going to pay off either, mostly due to bad weather which made fodder both scarce and expensive, these people had to unload cattle also and prices dropped drastically, showing once again how quickly markets can fluctuate. One get-rich-quick merchant, however, did very well for a while in America and the *Los Angeles Times* has kindly allowed me to let you into his secret, for though they do not claim to have invented the method, they do own the copyright of the tale as published by them in their issue of 11 May 1971.

Donkey Buyers Taken For A Ride

Everybody knew Silvio Deolindo De Carvalho – known as He of the Donkeys – sold some of the best horses and donkeys you could find.

The trouble was, say police, he sold them again and again, and again – the same donkeys and horses. He reputedly sold one donkey nine times – twice to the same buyer!

De Carvalho has denied the charges, but police will go ahead with the case.

When he was officially charged, more than 20 people turned up at the local police office where he was being held to press charges against him.

One of De Carvalho's top money winners, was a donkey called Ioio. This donkey was so fond of De Carvalho it would follow him everywhere. All he had to do was sell it, then pass by the house of the man to whom he had sold it. He did not have to steal Ioio back again. It recognized him and came trotting after him.

One man told police he bought the donkey, which was a very fine animal, but it disappeared soon afterwards. A long time later, De Carvalho told him he had another animal for sale, again a fine animal. But after he had bought it, the man realized it was the same animal he had bought the first time.

Trying to keep on the straight and narrow we prepared for our first sale in a very cowardly manner as some of the first donkeys to leave us went on lease and others were bought in to sell out again! As we had no wish to be dealers we soon stopped this latter operation and, when further would-be purchasers came along, we made a deal only when we believed the donkeys would be going to suitable homes. Only rarely have we ever parted with our adult stock and then for rather special reasons; but never again. We have decided that only the young must leave to face the quickly changing world; the others will grow old with us in our democratic donkey dominion. While asses galore may be what we wish, 'galore' must have a limit and wishes a limit also; and as we do not know of an oil-drenched sheik who is willing to pour his millions at our feet, change his priceless Cadillacs for these priceless asses, and keep us all in the style to which we would like to be accustomed, a few – only a few mind you – of our youngest will have to seek their fortunes elsewhere, as other youngsters have done successfully over the years.

Clonalis House, just outside Castlerea in County Roscommon and home of the O'Conors of Connacht, is one of the early places to which we delivered some donkeys: three youngsters called Jason, Lydia and Missy Miss. Here they thrive and receive plenty of attention as well as sharing an historic heritage, for the O'Conor Don, Chieftain of the Clan, is a descendant of the last High King of Ireland and the house is open to the public for whom its collection of ancient manuscripts, costumes and uniforms is an attraction.

Two broken-coloured youngsters, a colt and a filly, were bought by a lady under whose expert management they have won prizes at many shows, including the Dublin Horse Show at which one of them was chosen as Champion Donkey. Two geldings went to American friends who have a small holiday house nearby. When the owners are in residence, the donkeys are permitted on the lawn which they devour avidly, and they are now appropriately nicknamed Lawn and Mower! Another grey gelding, Doomsday, lives nearby too; he was purchased by a nun, home on holiday from America, for members of her family. Perhaps the most amusing name given to any of our outward bound stock is Bagpipes, who with his mother Clarionet also lives not far away.

Quite a few of our stallions have gone to the North of Ireland, one even suffering imprisonment en route. He had been sold for some weeks but the new owners had been unable to inform me when they would come and collect him. Returning from a walk quite late one evening I saw a vehicle almost the size of a pantechnicon outside our front door. Wondering whether my husband had at last had enough of us all and was about to move out, or whether someone wished to cart off the whole herd, I sped up the drive to find that it was our purchaser from the North come to collect merely one stallion and one mare! Speculations as to how we would load my poor beasts on to this great thingumajig without a crane, provided of course that I could get them from distant fields to the starting point without the help of my assistants who had gone off duty by then, ran riot in my head. I was also apprehensive as to how the donkeys were going to reach their destination without breaking every bone in their bodies, boomeranging from one wall of the huge van to the other, especially down Corkscrew Hill which was on their way. How we got the donkeys into that monstrosity I cannot begin to relate but, with the help of half the neighbourhood, we succeeded. Once inside things took a turn for the better, for with bedding, hay and above all some boards to act as partitions, the donkeys seemed to have a sporting chance of arriving at their destination safely. This possibility was further enhanced when we heard that, not planning to do the long journey at a stretch, the men were booked to stay in Galway for the night and the donkeys were bound for the county gaol!

Some years after that The Gossoon, a son of that character Betty Peg, also travelled north to a family in Newry. Almost as entertaining as his dam, he greatly enjoyed a bottle when a foal, and for ages afterwards the memory lingered on, so that when anyone came into a field he would canter up to them with his mouth wide open hee-hawing, still requesting the bottle.

To a delightful family in County Fermanagh went Franz Josef, the first bright-chestnut foal sired by our much mourned stallion Ard-Ri, with his grey/brown dam Sisi. His purchaser, arriving here first on a very wet day, got more than the usual share of entertainment provided for callers coming to see the donkeys. And though in all fairness I cannot say he applauded the act, neither can I say he was not vastly amused to see during the tour his middle-aged hostess, clad in wellingtons, mackintosh and sou'wester, fly through the air from the top of a high slippery bank to land spread-eagled face downwards in about six inches of mud. With hindsight – if under the circumstances I dare use such a word – I do not think Charlie Chaplin could have surpassed the performance. Peering through a film of mud I saw my rescuer gallantly wallow to my assistance, and having gingerly helped me uninjured from the slimy strata, we shook with mirth. A friendship, perhaps, cemented in mud!

One deal we made with a family who had previously bought some of our stock had a gambling flavour. A little white maiden-mare had got herself mated unofficially during a break-out, and we were not sure which stallion was responsible. If it was the chestnut Ard-Ri, she stood a chance of having a valuable pink foal, so we sold her at a 'middling-price'. Should the mare produce a pink foal, it would be a bargain for the new owners and, if a more usual-coloured one, a bargain for us. Well, a pink foal it was; the only pink foal he sired during his short life.

The bright chestnut colour is very popular at the moment, though not easy to come by. Of Ard-Ri's other two 'legitimate' foals, both from our chestnut mare Rowans, the filly Su Talon remains with us and the colt Craob Rua has gone to a lady in Dumfriesshire.

Many of our herd departed to reside in County Kerry, a mixed bag of ten to residents on one peninsula, two geldings to the American owners of lovely Killarney House and others to near the village of Sneem, where for twelve summers I had lived in the house later occupied by President de Gaulle on his visit to Ireland. And Tuppence, a foal, went to Charles, son of the famous racing trainer Vincent O'Brien.

Our first exports crossed the channel by air from Shannon and Dublin airports. They all went in pairs, side by side, head to tail in open-lathed wooden crates, which were fork-lifted on to the passenger planes. The first to go that way were a broken-coloured colt Cio and a gelding Ronco who, after excellent arrangements and a good flight, proceeded to their new home in Scotland by train. The second consignment met with a setback, for somewhere along the line our measurements went wrong and no amount of twisting, turning or squeezing would get the crate into the plane. I viewed the proceedings with dismay and embarrassment, as also did the passengers who were already in the plane, until a sorely tried pilot, perhaps envisaging an enlarging slice cut out of the side of his plane, bluntly told us all that he did not intend to have his whole schedule upset on account of two asses. So off flew the plane leaving those of us on terra firma in a fine dilemma. After much parlance it was decided that the crate could be cut down to the size required and, complete with the donkeys, could go off a few days hence. Meanwhile two officials who lived nearby would each kindly care for one of the donkeys. With these arrangements made we telephoned the news to the new owners who, poor souls, were already waiting at London airport. These two donkeys, a miniature stallion and a mare, were two of the very few attempts we made at buying-in donkeys for friends. We were thrilled later to see the stallion featuring on the jacket of a delightful book written by the owner.

Another airborne export had an expensive consequence. Two mares and a foal went to a young couple in Kent. The mare Patchwork, with her foal Petit Point accompanying her, was guaranteed in-foal again and carried a promise of £50 refund if this was not the case. Patchwork, however, failed to produce, which taught me a smart lesson, never to put my trust in 'them there lady asses' until almost the eleventh hour! The other mare was one of my favourites, Lotus. Kindly permitted into the plane to see them off, I was saying goodbye to her when she caught one end of my head scarf and held it firmly in her mouth. If I could have backed down on the deal honourably then and there I would have done. Apart from her sweet temperament Lotus had been a great pet due to our special attachment to her dam Echo, whose life we had saved with such difficulty when her tongue was paralysed for over two weeks.

Over the years our stock has gone by sea to England, Scotland, Holland and Australia. It took months of contemplation, discussion and negotiation before three of our adult miniature stock, a stallion Twill and two mares Lola and Ounce, set sail for Australia. The former two are broken-coloured animals and Ounce, who was in foal at the time, is brown. They had been sold seventeen months previously but it took the intervening time before arrangements could be made to suit vendors, purchasers and donkeys. From Spanish Point they went by trailer, rail, boat, rail, boat and trailer, the latter partly under police escort, until they reached their destination at Finnigan's Place, Ocean Grove, Victoria. The donkeys arrived appropriately enough on St Patrick's Day, with an extra member of the entourage, for a brown filly foal, Macushla, was born to Ounce during the long period in quarantine in Melbourne, this being longer than usual because of illness among some other animals on board.

A great welcome was prepared for the donkeys as news of their intended arrival had been broadcast over the radio in Geelong from a tape recording I had been asked to make. Although no one was allowed to come in contact with them as they disembarked, many people gathered to see these small, unusual-coloured little asses who had travelled half-way across the world. When they left quarantine for the last sixty miles of their journey by road to Ocean Grove, the donkeys got VIP treatment with reporters, photographers and radio and television teams covering their trail. Visitors, including many Irish people, came to see the new arrivals happily ensconced in and around Leprechaun Lodge, a thatched shelter built especially for them, at the now-established Finnigan Irish Donkey Stud, owned by John and Justyne Finnigan.

It was because of their ability not only to stand extreme heat, but to flourish in it, that donkeys were first imported to Australia as working animals around the end of the eighteenth century. With the arrival of mechanisation the asses became redundant and were left loose in a climate so conducive to their welfare that they bred ceaselessly until, in both the Northern and Western Territory, they became so numerous as to be declared vermin. Then evolved what must surely be one of the greatest tragedies in animal history, the annual slaughter of thousands upon thousands of donkeys by a diversity of frightful methods, in an effort to exterminate them. It is heartening to know that many people in Australia are now doing their best to save these lovely creatures by starting societies and clubs devoted entirely to the promotion of their welfare. In such photographs of them as I have seen, they look handsome animals. I hear that the great majority of them stand between 44 and 52in high and are used as riding donkeys by adults as well as children. Nevertheless there is a strong interest in the miniatures too, so the smaller breed of donkey we sent over has retained its great welcome.

For many years I have had a very special feeling that 'donkey contact' would prove to be natural medicine in the field of therapeutics. When I wrote my first book and stated this belief for the first time in print, I did not dare to hope, still less assume, that experts in this line of work would welcome our long-eared friend as an assistant, or that interest would have become so widespread so soon. We have been privileged to supply several hospitals, homes and societies in Ireland, who care especially for both physically and mentally handicapped children, with pairs of specially selected animals. I am very glad to hear that, so far, they are plodding along most helpfully.

Our donkeys have company from birth, which is why we send them off in pairs. In general it is true with animals, as with humans, that those who have company of their own sort are vastly contented and relaxed, and these virtues are most necessary when in contact with young, especially autistic, children. This venture, one that is very close to all our hearts here, has aroused much home and overseas interest and, judging by those who call and write to us about it, the interest is growing apace. The German Donkey Society in their magazine, *Esel Revue*, published an erudite article on this subject by Dr Werner Fritz Ebel from Berlin, and the English Donkey Breed Society's magazine has also written on this topic.

Dr Patrick Power, in charge of Our Lady's Hospital in Ennis, County Clare, which, under his direction, was the first hospital to countenance keeping donkeys for the benefit of its patients, has sent me the following report of their value in this field:

> Donkey riding gave the children a great deal of pleasure. They made vital contact with the donkeys which they are often unable to experience with people and were rewarded with satisfaction instead of frustration.
>
> Though the patients showed much apprehension at first, some needing three helpers (one leading, two offering support) now one-third of them can sit without support and will soon be hacking under supervision. In the future we hope to introduce games, eg throwing objects into a bucket as they ride past and simple obstacle races. Riding offers the children the opportunity of participating in a normal play activity, exposing the mentally subnormal child to many experiences of outdoor life he/she could not otherwise have experienced and enjoyed. The warmth, motion and physical contact with

the donkey helps to bring out the withdrawn child, and behaviour problems, such as outbursts of aggression are reduced.

From a socialising point of view, the fact that the child can participate helps him/her to develop self-confidence, particularly when he/she receives recognition from others. Support is gained from the group experience of being accepted and the child learns to accept others. By looking after and feeding the donkeys a sense of responsibility is instilled in the child. Physically riding is an excellent form of exercise – strengthens trunk and back muscles, educates balance and gives confidence and develops controlled movement. The results from riding, for these children in terms of pleasure and personal achievement, apart from the remedial value, were dramatic.

That the donkey has contributed in any way, however slight, to the dedicated work carried out amongst these sadly afflicted patients, shows once again that he is continuing to play his humble, though invaluable rôle in the life of man.

10 Our Duty to Animals

Successful living between all beings depends on a give and take relationship, both physical and mental. The greater the attention given to this relationship, the more rewarding will be the result when dealing with both humans and animals. We get to know the likes and dislikes of our loved ones and friends by observation, and do what we can for their welfare, trusting that they will do the same for us. For a human relationship to develop, an understanding of each other's limitations and potential is necessary, as well as common willingness to weigh the balance at all times. Although on a different level, the human-animal relationship should run along similar lines, at the same time making allowances for those superior gifts that are allocated only to mankind.

The widely-held belief that many animals, including donkeys, are stupid, is a fallacy. These creatures have an awareness of certain dangers which is hidden from man, yet they fail to comprehend many things which seem obvious to their human owners, and thus fall prey to the visible dangers caused by man's negligence. The donkey's innate curiosity also gets him into trouble, so if you want to own your donkeys for a long time, you must do some smart thinking before letting them loose in your world. Let your imagination work overtime and, when you have thought of all the things you should do to ensure his wellbeing, you will still not be half-way there, as the things you must *not* do will keep you busy for a long time yet. 'What, pit my genius against a donkey!' you say condescendingly. Say it if you must, but do not bet on who will win! Just concentrate on making friends with your animals to start with, handle them, talk to them and give them confidence in your gentleness. Then it will be much easier to discipline them later on and you will be able to contend with them in any startling situation that may arise.

Man's obligation to put humanitarian principles into practice when dealing with inferior and dependent creatures rests on the same basis as all other moral obligations, regardless of religious creeds – a sense of what is right and just. Yet there are many people of true benevolence and humanity to their fellow men who seem unconscious that these considerations should be extended to the animal creation. Perhaps this want of sympathy is merely a lack of understanding of a subject which formed no part of their early education and has never been brought before them as a moral consideration.

It is surely important that children should be instructed, both at home and in school, in a knowledge of animals, most especially the domestic ones to which we are indebted for innumerable benefits. Naturally, all children will not have the same interest in and affection for animals, but they could be taught to care and respect those which contribute in so many different ways to our comfort and well-being. Indeed animals and young children resemble each other in some ways, in that the stream of feeling is always there, whereas their judgement is fitful and requires channelling. Perhaps our children when taught to have solicitude for animals, might more easily learn to understand and tolerate that higher animal, man himself, for 'just as the twig is bent, the tree's inclined'. And perhaps those of them who say their prayers at bedtime could add the same solemn request to the

Almighty as did Albert Schweitzer, when as a little boy he prayed with his mother before going to sleep, 'O good Lord, protect and bless all things that breathe, preserve all living things from evil and suffer them to sleep in peace . . .'

In the second century AD Marcus Aurelius Antoninus, an emperor of Rome before Christianity became acceptable there, writes in the record of his spiritual life: 'To receive inward impressions of external things is given even to the beasts of the field.' Earlier still Triptolemus, the first Athenian legislator, made few laws but three are recorded: 'Honour your parents; worship the Gods; hurt not animals.'

From a Christian point of view it must be obvious that He who said: 'Are not five sparrows sold for two farthings, and not one of them is forgotten in the sight of God' could never have meant that the animal creation should be excluded from the influence of His mercy. For although the Almighty gave man '. . . dominion over every living thing that moveth on the earth' (Genesis, CI, v28), it must surely have been a delegated trust which man is required to carry out with discretion and lenity, and not to violate.

Christianity is throughout a religion of mercy, not limited to any people or nation, nor to the sphere of rationality itself, but extending to the extreme limit of life and sense. All through Holy Writ there is frequent mention of various animals to illustrate the divine teachings. His discourses are illustrated with incomparable beauty by allusions to external nature and images taken from the vegetable and animal kingdoms; to draw attention to them all would fill pages. Suffice it to say that we might reasonably conclude that no animal should be an object of contempt much less of inhumanity. As C. S. Lewis writes: 'They are our fellow-dependents; we all, lions, storks, ravens, whales – live, as our fathers said 'at God's charges', and mention of all equally redounds to his praise.'

The role of teacher need not be a one-sided affair. Job, for instance, knew that animals have a lot to teach us: 'Ask now the beasts and they shall teach thee; and the fowls of the air and they shall tell thee; or the reptiles of the earth and they shall inform

OUR DUTY TO ANIMALS

thee' (c12, v7-8). And Alexander Pope has caught and amplified the idea with his usual felicity:

> Go: from the creatures thy instructions take:
> Learn from the birds what food the thickets yield;
> Learn from the beasts the physic of the field;
> Thy arts of building from the bee receive,
> Learn of the mole to plough, the worm to weave.

Nature is often the best instructor and reason may profit by the tuition of instinct. Those who have lived with animals and studied them know that, as well as instincts, they have many senses and impulses in common with humans. We know that, like us, animals suffer physical pain from injury, disease and in the bringing forth of their young, but do we sufficiently consider their sensations of hunger, thirst, heat, cold, fear, anger, loneliness, confinement, loyalty, affection, joy, their maternal instincts and the strong conjugal feelings possessed by some of them? Their joys and contentment are obvious in the individual sounds of their species – bird songs, the purr of a cat, the enchanting snuffly noises made by donkeys when those they know and like appear, are but a few of the cheerful animal noises that are easily discernible. But an animal in distress or want is not so easily, or sometimes so willingly, perceived and, as it cannot utter its complaints in articulate sounds and has no earthly tribunal to witness its wrongs, it is left to people of compassionate nature to attempt to right these wrongs.

The sad thing is that many educated people think it is too soft and silly to bother about what happens to animals or to set a good example to the persons less well-educated, who perhaps have had little time to read and have never thought seriously about such things. It is when we find that someone who, tired and hungry, has had to work with his animals for his daily bread, yet treats them with consideration, that the true meaning of 'kindness to animals' is apparent. To those of us who keep them only as pets, it should be an accepted responsibility.

Do we make any endeavour to see that our money-spinning

horses, prize-winning animals or faithful companions have an honourable retirement or peaceful end to their lives? Do we really feel it our duty to care about their rights or do we leave it all to others to see to it for us? As long as these animals pay us well financially or in kind, is that all we care? Much can be done in small ways, such as questioning the motives of those who own dogs and cats as pets or 'home appendages', leaving them locked in or tied up unnecessarily for long hours unattended, or dropping them from cars miles from home when tired of them. Remonstrate with those who cram cattle or sheep into overcrowded trucks and trailers, who capture and keep birds in tiny cages, who injure animals when driving on the roads and do not stop to care for them, or commit the many acts of thoughtless cruelty which we all know are of common occurence.

When we come across such cruelties, have not the animals the right to rely on us to protest? Why in this so-called enlightened age, with a vast choice of the ways and means to find pleasure, is it necessary to subject animals to an agonising death for our amusement as is done in bull-fighting, live hare coursing, organised shoots or shooting for fun by bad marksmen and, with the growth of scientific knowledge, is it really necessary these days to subject animals to vivisection?

Agreeing that we have the right to kill certain animals and to eat them, in order to preserve nature's balance, have we in the western world not enough variety on our menu without the luxuries gained by the cruel and unnatural ways of fattening poultry and treating young creatures for the table? Do we make it our business to find out if the beasts we eat have been dispatched in a humane manner and that our abbatoirs, especially the rural ones, are run without cruelty?

One of the many valued contributions which we constantly receive from visitors to the stud, was found between the pages of our visitors' book, unsigned and almost illegible. I hope we have made it out correctly as being:

> A man of kindness to his beast is kind,
> But a brutal action shows a brutal mind.

OUR DUTY TO ANIMALS

Beast can't complain, but God's all-seeing eye
Beholds the cruelty and notes the cry.

And it is certainly not fanciful to believe that the Almighty's eye fell even on the humble donkey, as mention of the ass appears in *The Bible* in connection with some of the most important people and events of those days. As we all know, it is even mentioned by name in one of the ten commandments. Our quadruped appears again and again throughout the Scriptures until his day of days when he carried Christ into Jerusalem on Palm Sunday. Nowhere in the Bible do we hear of the ass being derided or abused; on the contrary we learn that his wants were carefully considered and his services greatly valued. His characteristics were observed with comprehension and he was thought to be the only animal endowed with the gift of foresight. The mystery is why, over the centuries, he has had to bear more than his share of the burdens and follies of the world.

When numbers and dimensions are enormous, as in the variety of cruelties committed by mankind not only against animals but against their fellow men, it is understandable for an individual to boggle at the thought of how little he or she can do to make the effort worthwhile or make any impression at all. When such a thought comes my way, I think on the phrase that ends each verse of a children's hymn – 'you in your small corner and I in mine'. I seldom hear the hymn now and I cannot remember all the verses, only the strong impression it made on me as a child and which I still retain, to the effect that each one of us must try to shine a light in our own small corner against the darkness of the world, so that some day all the lights together can dispel that darkness. Reflections on this can aid our feeling of futility when the assistance we can tender in any catastrophic event seems puny, and the mite we offer seems overwhelmed by the millions required. We cannot alone defeat the powers of darkness, and who is to say which corner is darkest, but one tiny light could show those in nearby corners where to find the matches and to discover in which direction their lights should shine.

OUR DUTY TO ANIMALS

Before considering keeping any animal, we must, therefore, be fully aware of our moral obligations towards it. On a more practical level, when people who know little about horses or donkeys are thinking of owning one for the first time, it is helpful for them to know the primary essentials for its welfare before they do so. A list of instructions that read like an invoice are not only very boring but also difficult to remember. So joining my apologies to Rudyard Kipling with those of the many others who have already strained his famous poem to cover many a subject, I now add *Equus asinus* to the list.

If you would own an ass, then treat him kindly
    And learn about the things that you must do.
To keep him well, contented and not blindly
    Leave him neglected and dejected too.

If you can have a place where he can shelter
    From winter gales, sharp icy hail and snow;
An airy shed for those times when it swelters.
    For weather's wiles can be his greatest foe.

Some enemies so real they must be mentioned,
    Are parasites in him and on the sward.
Strict dosing, pasture changes; these attentions
    Will bring the ass – the owner – its reward.

If you can get the blacksmith when he's needed,
    To keep your asses hooves pared, neat and trim,
Though if his daily work is on the highway,
    He'll soon require a shoe to guard their rim.

If you are ill you need to see a doctor,
    An animal's a living creature too.
So if he's ill, though you can act as proctor,
    The vet is trained, and knows a thing or two.

If time to spare you groom his coat minutely,
    And clean right through until you reach the hide,
For should there be a host of foreign bodies
    Left undisturbed, your donkey will not thrive.

OUR DUTY TO ANIMALS

We all have taste, the ass is no exception.
  Of pure, fresh water he must have his fill.
So understand this asinine perception,
  As drinking dirty water's not his will.

If grass is scarce, some hay will go down nicely,
  Nuts, oats and maize will serve the self-same end.
If company as well you have provided,
  You qualify – to own an ass my friend.

I close with the fervent wish that, along our coastal roads, and in any other treeless or hedgeless areas where animals are exposed to the whims of the elements, a wall-cross of stones should be constructed. Built as shown in the illustration below, with some gravel or shingle on the bottom to act as drainage they would, at least, take the brunt of the lashing winds, rain or hailstones, especially the latter which can stick in an animal's coat, melt and trickle through to the skin, making the poor beast colder than ever. And in summer too, these wall-crosses would be useful, giving a certain amount of shade from the heat of the sun. Remnants of them are still to be seen here and there, but seldom more than this.

Index

Aberdeen Arms Hotel, 105
abuse, 10, 131
Aelian, 98
agapanthus, 69
age, 9
Agnew, Hon Mrs E., 6
Agricultural Institute, 46
Alana, 67, 68, 80, 92
Alpine flowers, 12
America, 113
Americans, 77, 78, 90, 106
American Council of Spotted Asses, 105
American Donkey and Mule Society, 105
Animal Health Trust, 26
Antoninus, Marcus Aurelius, 128
Ard-Ri, 31, 120, 121
Aristotle, 14
Armada, 12
Assile, 103
Atlantic gales, 13, 79
Atlantic kelp, 46
Atlas countries, 113
Australia, 13, 122, 123, 124
autistic, 124
autopsy, 43, 44

Bagpipes, 119
Ballsbridge, 104
Barker, Noel, 28, 76, 77
batty, 116
behaviour, 9, 10
Betty-Peg, 19, 32, 120
Bible, 127; biblical, 60
blacksmith, 16, 77, 132
Blue-tit, 98
Bord Failte, 64
Breaffy, 49, 50, 55-7, 59
breeding, 13, 14
British Isles, 10, 13
brochure, 66, 89
broken-coloured, 38, 54, 61, 116, 117, 119
Brown, Thomas, 40
Buffon, M. du, 41
bull-fighting, 130
Bungie, 96
Burren, 12
bus-loads, 64, 65, 72, 71-3

Cambrian Airways, 85
carelessness, 35
Caro, 53
cart, 10, 91, 101
catering, 82-4
cats, 96
champion donkey, 104
Chardin, Teilhardin de, 94
chestnut colouring, 81

Childers, Erskine, President of Ireland, and his wife Rita, 76, 79, 80, 81
chill, 32, 38
Christianity, 128
chums, 17
Cio, 121
Clare, 12, 100, 124
Clare Champion, the, 99
Clarionet, 119
Cledagh, 22, 31, 32
Cliffs of Moher, 12
climate, 13, 14, 37-9, 41, 76, 77, 79
Clonalis House, 119
Cloud, 50
clover, 44, 47
colostrum, 56
companionship, 22, 25, 54, 133
condition, 14
Congested District Board, 38
Coral, 77, 136
correspondence, 99, 103, 109
cow-hocks, 112, 113
Craob Rua, 121
crates, 121
crosses, 98, 99
cruelty, 102, 130
curiosity, 11, 126

Deakin, John, 49ff
dehydration, 26
Delaney's Donkey, 64
diarrhoea, *see* scouring
diet, 36ff
discomfort dance, 42, 46, 58
donkey diary, 41
Donkey Shop, 64, 71
Doomsday, 119
Doonagore, 59
droppings, *see* faeces
Dubh'sban, 50, 53
Dublin, 43, 67, 106, 121
Dublin Horse Show, 103, 104, 119
Dubourdieu, 38

Ebel, Dr Werner Fritz, 124
Echo, 122
Edwardian, 10
England, 62, 122
English Donkey Breed Society, 122
English National Coal Board, 84
Ennis, 100, 106, 124
Ennistymon, 32
environment, 13
Epstein, H., 113
equus asinus, 6, 15, 94, 105, 112
Esel-Revue, 124
extra-legs, 92

INDEX

faeces, 27, 44, 47
Fairview Lady, 104
Fermanagh, 120
fertilisers, 41, 42, 44, 46
Finnigan's Place, 124; John and Justyne, 123
foaling, 21–4, 27–9
foals, 20–4, 42, 46, 77
Foreign Minister, 68
fore-legs, 93, 94, 112
Franz Josef, 120
freemartinism, 60
French farmers, 78
Friendship Table, 91

gales, 13, 132
Galway, 120
gaol, 120
gelding, 50, 54
German, caravan-rally, 78; Donkey Society, 124; golfers, 78; police, 78
Georgina (Wilde), 92
gestation, 19
Gossoon, The, 120
Granny Velvet, 78, 80
Gray, David, 104

habitat, 11, 13
habits, 14
Hall, Frank, 63
hares, 96, 97, 130
hay, 10, 36, 47, 77
hay-bag, 31
Hayes, Captain, 93
Heber, Reginald, Bishop of Calcutta, 112
herbage, 40, 41, 43, 44, 108
Hillery, Dr Patrick, 66, 67
hocks, 112
Holland, 122
hooves, 17, 32, 56, 77, 92–4, 112, 132
Horrible Dog, 95–7
horse, 10, 16, 37, 41, 47, 94, 106, 111, 112
'Horses', 93
Houdini, 32
hybrids, 113
hymn, 131

Ireland, 11, 37, 81, 85, 98, 116, 119, 124
'Irish Donkey, The', 64
Irish Donkey Society, 98, 99, 102–4, 106, 112, 117, 118,
Irish holiday, 85
Irish Lace (Lacy), 30
Irish Penny Magazine, 41
International Encyclopedia of Veterinary Medicine (1966), 60
intussusception, 43

jackdaws, 97
Jason, 119
Job, 128
judges, 104–6

Kerry, 39, 121
Killarney, 85
Killarney House, 121
King Jacko, 104

Kingsley-Lewis, Daphne, 109
Kipling, Rudyard, 132

Lahinch, 105
lameness, 42
Lawn, 119
lawn-mowings, 47
Leprechaun Lodge, 123
Lewis, C. A., 128
Limerick, 61, 72
Lisdoonvarna, 19
Lola, 122
Londonderry, 38
'long-eared buns', 105
Los Angeles Times, 6, 117
Lotus, 122
Lydia, 119
Lyne, Michael, 104

MacNamara, Colonel Thomas, 81
magpie, 98
Malaga, 38
mating, 18, 19, 26
McNeill, 38
meconium, 57
Medina House, 17
Melbourne, 123
Middle East, 108
miniature, 122, 123
Miss Bonny, 53
Miss Rockefeller, 80
Missy Miss, 119
Mister Ister, 96
Mitchell, Mrs Murray, 102
Money Moon, 24, 80
Montana, 105
Mower, 119
Murray, J. P., 98

nettle-roots, 41
negligence, 125
Nickel, 22–4
night-watch, 27, 29
Northern Ireland, 49, 119–21

obligations, 127, 132
O'Brien, Vincent, 117
O'Connor, Don, 119
Oklahoma, 79
Ome, Omi, 56–9, 78
O'Moore, L. B., 6, 46
opening-day, 68
O'Reilly, 50
orphan foal, 25, 74
Ounce, 122
Our Lady's Hospital, 124
O'Shannon, Cathal, 63

Paddy Medina, 92–4, 101
Palm Sunday, 131
Parker, David J., 105
parrot-mouth, 108
Patchwork, 122
Pegeen, 46
Pepito, 54, 62, 63
Petit Point, 122
pets, 11, 129, 130

INDEX

placenta, 26, 56
plantain, 41, 47
Pluche, Abbe la, 41
Points of the Horse, 93
Pope, Alexander, 129
Portrush, 50
post-mortem, *see* autopsy
Power, Dr Patrick, 6, 124
prolapse, 44
provoking, 29
Pythagorean, 57

Rainbow, 19, 31, 92
Rainbow Donkey Sweaters, 86, 89
Ras Shamra, 27, 28, 80, 92
'rear-end skid', 21
refreshments, 64–6, 84
remuneration, 116
riding, 107, 123–5
Rita, 81
Rome, 128
Ronco, 121
Roscommon, 39, 120
Royal Dublin Society (RDS), 38, 103, 105

Schweitzer, Albert, 128
scouring, 26, 42, 59
Scotland, 122
Scott, Mrs, 104
Shackleton, Muriel, 104
shelters, 14, 16, 132, 133
Shron Dubh, 94
Shubad, 40, 80, 92
Simpson, George Gaylord, 93
singly, 27
Sisi, 27, 120
slaughter, 123
souvenirs, 86
Spanish ass, 38
Spanish Point, 12, 66, 78, 100, 122
stallions, 18, 19, 27, 49, 50, 73, 109
Stanley, Richard, 104
Stephens, James, 36
stupidity, 9, 126
substitute feeding, 24–6
sucking, 24, 25
surprise-packets, 67, 105
suspended animation, 27
Su Talun, 120

swing, 31

television, 62, 63
tetanus, 26
therapeutic, 6, 124
thermometer, 74
Tommyduffy, 39, 40
Tourist Board, *see* Bord Failte
trade, 117
trailer, 32, 54, 83
transportation, 16, 130
Tuppence, 121
Turf, 28
turf (peat), 10
turf-baskets, 67
Twill, 122
Twinnies, *see* Ome, Omi
twins, 39, 40, 60
'tying the knot', 45

ulcers, 43, 45
umbilical cord, 26, 27
USA, 13
USA Democratic Party, 90

Vaysse, 113
Ventromil, 45, 59
vet, 17, 21, 22, 26, 30, 59, 132
Victorian, 10
vivisection, 130

wall-cross, 133
wall, stone, 12
warts, 30
water, 29, 133
weather, 72, 76, 77, 117
White Ass Inn, 85, 86
Whiteford, Kathleen, 92
wild ass, 11, 39, 109, 113, 114
Wilson II, Carl A., 105
wind, 12, 41, 76, 97
work, 10
Wylie, John E., 104, 106

Yorkshire, 84

zebra, 54, 94, 109
zoo, 40, 41, 49, 50
Zoo (Benvarden), 53, 54